Vision Driven

Lessons Learned from the Small Business C-Suite

Mallary Tytel, Ph.D., M.B.A.

Gold Canyon Press

To contact the author with comments or to inquire about speaking, coaching or consulting, write to her at: mtytel@healthyworkplaces.com

The opinions expressed in this manuscript are solely the opinions of the author and do not represent the opinions or thoughts of the publisher. The author has represented and warranted full ownership and/or legal right to publish all the materials in this book.

Author's Note: The narratives in this book reflect actual events. The names and genders of those individuals cited in these stories have been changed for reasons of privacy.

Vision Driven
Lessons Learned from the Small Business C-Suite
All Rights Reserved.
Copyright © 2009 Mallary Tytel, Ph.D., M.B.A.
V12.0

Cover Photo © 2009 JupiterImages Corporation. All rights reserved - used with permission.

This book may not be reproduced, transmitted, or stored in whole or in part by any means, including graphic, electronic, or mechanical without the express written consent of the publisher except in the case of brief quotations embodied in critical articles and reviews.

Gold Canyon Press
P.O. Box 2223
Apache Junction, Arizona 85217-2223
U.S.A.
www.goldcanyonpress.com

www.vision-driven.net

PB ISBN: 978-0-9821112-0-8

Library of Congress Control Number: 2008936619

PRINTED IN THE UNITED STATES OF AMERICA

To Stephen, Jessica and Bradley, who matter most.

TABLE OF CONTENTS

Acknowledgments ix

Introduction: The First Day on the Job xi

Part I. The Vision 1
   1.   Understanding your Organization 3
   2.   Defining Leadership 7
   3.   Strategic Planning 11
   4.   Developing the Management Team 15
   5.   Managing Change 21
   6.   The Three B's of Quality 23
   7.   Thinking About the Future 27
   8.   Measuring Results: The Balanced Scorecard 31
   9.   Smile! 35
  10.   Customer Experience Management 39
  11.   Managers as Leaders 45
  12.   Preparing for the Unknown 47
  13.   A Framework for Action 51
  14.   What Matters Most 53

Part II. The Lessons 57
  15.   The Personal Equation 59
  16.   Maintaining the Helm 61
  17.   Ideas Anyone? 65
  18.   The Whole Package 69
  19.   The 10-Minute Rule 73
  20.   The Good News and the Bad News 79
  21.   Rumor's Had It! 81

22.	What is at Risk?	87
23.	Managing 360 Degrees	89
24.	It's Lonely at the Top	93
25.	Hats Off to HR!	97
26.	Separate the Message from the Messenger	99
27.	It's Not Personal, It's Business; It's Not Business, It's Personal	103
28.	Saying Goodbye is as Important as Saying Hello	111
29.	Evaluation: The Partner of Effective Decision Making	115
30.	How Many Decisions Did You Make Today?	123
31.	Culture Is	125
32.	Culture Comes from the Top	127
33.	Capacity	133
34.	Don't Forget to Ask How YOU are Doing	137
35.	Accountability Counts	141
36.	Glory Days	147
37.	Jockeying for Position	149
38.	Seek out Opportunities and People to Laugh With	153
39.	Controversy in the Workplace	159
40.	A Matter of Balance	161
41.	You Bring More to Work than Your Lunch: One Example	163
42.	Keeping Yourself in the Feedback Loop	167
43.	Uncivil Service	171
44.	Rituals	175
45.	Managing Time	177
46.	Call a Time Out	181
47.	Making a Difference: A Parable	185
48.	There's No "I" in March Madness	189
49.	Dialogue for One	195
50.	Total Quality Leadership	199

51.	Gifts of the Season	203
52.	Matters of the Heart	205
53.	Caution: Leadership Ahead	209
54.	Supervisors, Be All You Can Be	213
55.	The Contract Compact	217
56.	Recognition	221
57.	The 100th Monkey: A Story About Social Change	225
58.	Knowledge Management	229
59.	The Pick of the Litter	233
60.	So, How Are You?	237
61.	Simple Rules	241
62.	Asking the Questions	245
63.	Performance Art	249
64.	Business Partners	253
65.	Rules of Engagement	257
66.	Time Off	261
67.	Help Thyself	265
68.	Learning in Action	269
69.	So You Want to Be an Entrepreneur	273
Part III.	The Big Picture	277
70.	Picking Yourself Up	279
71.	Here's to What's Next	283
72.	Know Thyself	287
73.	Being There	291
74.	The Big Picture	295
75.	Vision Driven	299
Selected References		301

ACKNOWLEDGMENTS

It is with great appreciation and affection that I recognize and express my thanks to those individuals who provided their time, energy and wisdom to making this book a reality.

Glenna Garcia, for her sincere candor, her proficiency in guiding the book through production and for being there;

Leah Shepherd, for her expert editing, her crisp comments and her thoughtful advice;

Royce Holladay, for her creative brilliance, her solid grounding and her vast editorial know-how;

Cathy Perme, for her keen abilities, for bearing witness and her honest friendship;

Gail Champlin, for her exceptional capacity to give, her incisive ability to listen and her gift for grasping the big picture;

Kelly Walters-Kennedy, for her strength, her own far-reaching vision and for believing;

Dr Glenda Eoyang, for her genius, her unbounded passion and her steadfast commitment to asking questions;

The many small business and nonprofit professionals and colleagues who shared with me their own stories and lessons learned; and

The enormously talented and dedicated individuals it was my honor to work with side-by-side every day.

INTRODUCTION
The First Day on the Job

"It's what you learn after you know it all that counts."
John Wooden

Within the space of two weeks I left my position of seven years working under contract for the Department of the Army; helped clean out and organize our house in Maryland which was being sold; found and rented a temporary apartment in Connecticut; packed an assortment of my personal and professional belongings; drove 280 miles to my rented apartment; and prepared to start a new job.

On a holiday Monday at noon, Roberta, my new assistant, met me at the office. Going over many housekeeping details, she handed me a set of keys and took me on a brief tour of the facilities. While she and I walked around the floor, her husband, Keith, and my husband, Stephen, were left to chat. When she and I returned and they left, I asked Stephen what the two of them had talked about. "Nothing," he said. "He was afraid to say the wrong thing. After all, you're the new boss. You hold their future in your hands."

I thought about that for a long time. Me? Of course I was aware of my responsibility and authority. Upon hiring, my mandate from the board of directors was to "(re)position the company for the future" as the current CEO was stepping down.

I knew I'd have to make more difficult decisions than easy ones, plan and carry out more complex tasks than simple ones and implement significant change in an environment that was deeply rooted in the past. I was also prepared at any moment to be held accountable for everything. Well, it goes with the territory.

However, the truth was that he was only half right. We each held the others' future in our hands. Throughout my entire tenure at that organization I never forgot that. It was not them or me, though there were times when it seemed like it. It was *us*. Lesson No. 1.

* * * * *

The purpose of this book is to offer a kaleidoscope of snapshots into the everyday workings of leading and managing small organizations. This book is not simply about one particular assignment or environment, but the learning, development and growth that emerge from small-business management experiences, particularly in the nonprofit sector. Every organization is different. Yet the skills, talents and wisdom that are necessary for success are common to all enterprises.

Being a CEO – or even upper-level officer or manager – is often a larger-than-life position and filled with questions that aren't answered in an MBA education. Every challenge has multiple solutions, each of which can be right and wrong in a given situation. Therefore it is the questions and context we must pay attention to, and more often than not, that is where our learning comes from.

Let me assure you that your craziness in the job is understood; there are others out there who share your angst. For example, I recall during the first months of my tenure as CEO I harbored a nagging suspicion that at any moment the CEO-police would come crashing into my office, pointing at me in indignation and shouting, "Out Imposter!" I took it upon myself to become quite knowledgeable about the imposter syndrome and learned that (1) I was not alone; (2) this phenomenon is thought to be more common among women; (3) it seems to affect individuals who are actually successful rather than those who are not; and (4) it passes. This turned out to be another lesson learned.

In this book I offer some fundamental insights about your greatest and most common challenges. This is served as discerning food for thought based upon my experiences and the research and practice of others. You can use them today or tomorrow to address your persistent dilemmas.

I have deliberately chosen the format of vignettes. Each brief self-contained narrative offers a situation that focuses on the moment at hand. Opportunities for learning often sneak up on us or come out of the simplest exchanges of words or deeds. They are all pieces of the whole and as the picture emerges so, too, do patterns and the chance to act.

We have all taken advantage of teachable moments. By stopping and examining an event in the moment, we create our own lessons learned. In addition, each of these stories ends with a question. They are triggers for your own ideas, adding a reflective as well as informative activity for consideration. Sometimes in the most complex environments things are often less complicated than they seem. That is where common sense and clear thinking are more important than lots of models and theories.

The book is divided into three parts.

Part One is The Vision.

Anyone who steps into a leadership role or stands at the helm of an organization, particularly when there has been a long and rich history before you appeared on the scene, understands that you are essentially taking on three distinct entities. The first is the organization of today: doing business as usual, maintaining customers, contracts, obligations, commitments and quality.

The second is the organization of tomorrow: that which will emerge based on your vision, goals, efforts and ideas. That organization will successfully meet the challenges and opportunities of the shifting business landscape. It is what you aspire to. Finally, the third is the organization that is in transition, moving from the here and now into the future. This encompasses change, growth, development and integrity of mission and commitment to your constituents and stakeholders. Oh, yes, and resistance, too.

Your Vision is the basis of all that you do. It creates a foundation, sets the stage and informs others about who you are and the purpose and meaning that you bring to and share with your organization. Jonathan Swift said, "Vision is the art of seeing the invisible." This is at one and the same time a mystery and it is crystal clear. It is what you carry around with you wherever you are, whatever you do, what you see fixed on the horizon.

Part Two is Lessons Learned.

The day-to-day management and operations of the organization provide a dynamic canvas whereby the common trials and triumphs of the workplace and its members can be viewed and assessed. From the daily course of doing business, we can take the expected, unexpected, intended and unintended consequences of our actions and create a body of knowledge known as "lessons learned."

Perhaps more familiar in government and military environments, the notion of lessons learned speaks to that knowledge that comes from the implementation and evaluation of a program, project or process. This knowledge is gained empirically rather than by expertise. It identifies and highlights the incremental, innovative and measurable improvements for the organization. Taking advantage of lessons learned supports the replication of successful outcomes while eliminating unsuccessful outcomes.

In selecting the accounts for Part Two, I concentrated on significance, relevance, the relationships involved and the connection of the circumstances to the whole system. Lessons learned are not only a critical piece of an organizational culture that is committed to change. The true value and eventual payoff come in transforming *lessons learned* into *lessons applied*.

Part Three is The Big Picture.

When I was a girl in school we would hear much about our "permanent records." Nerdy kids like me acted with great care and concern because we knew that any mishap or misstep would be placed in our permanent records – forever a blot upon our fair names and fine characters. It was only with time, experience and a bit of wisdom that I recognized that the random misadventures of children did not speak to the sum total of who and what we are. The whole of each of us and all that we do are greater than the sum of our parts. We can choose to fixate on each wrinkle that presents itself or open our mind's eye to the abundant and broad cloth of experience and wonder that make up the entirety of our world.

So, too, it is in our work. We each stand within our own landscapes. It is through an awareness, examination and analysis of the panorama of behaviors, trends and patterns around us that we can clearly view our organizations, their activities and processes. It is a shift within our heads.

The big picture may represent a particular circumstance or issue or the entire enterprise; it may also include the individual, the organization or the entire community. More importantly, it allows us to see ourselves from a systemic stance, in relation to others and our environment. Context matters and this is where we move from our feet planted firmly on the ground to a vantage point of 25,000 feet in the air.

By the way, I think all of our permanent records are now available on the Internet.

Finally, if we really think about it, we recognize that everywhere we turn we are amidst complex systems. These systems, such as corporations, communities, families, Girl Scout troops and alumni associations, have characteristics that influence the whole and whose parts are connected and interdependent. Since our systems are open, they are subject to outside influences such as time, space, market crises, political world events and Mother Nature. As such, the system and those who are part of it – us! – must in our own individual and collective ways respond to our environments.

To say the whole is greater than the sum of its parts is only the beginning of understanding. For example, a new work group comes together on a special project. There are introductions, shaking hands and getting-to-know-you conversations. These are soon replaced with agendas, schedules and brainstorms. Order evolves, as does a plan, assignments and project timeline. Through organization of processes and procedures – however that happens – tasks are accomplished, deadlines are met, deliverables are completed and a new product is launched. Successful outcomes all around and yet beyond the individual and the whole is the greater whole: interdependencies are identified and influenced; alliances are developed; bonds are created; relationships are recognized and appreciated; new patterns are formed. From all of this motion and commotion, something fresh and sound, vibrant and important, has emerged.

When we stand in this new and different space, with a broader point of view, we can begin to grasp all that is in front of us. Our means are interpretation, implication and then application. That is when we can understand the influence of the environment and those around us; set and guide the behavior of others; and know what is important. By identifying the patterns that make up our world, we can influence and inform the paths to innovation, collaboration and participation.

And we can lead.

PART I
The Vision

"If you want to build a ship, don't drum up people to collect wood and don't assign them tasks and work, but rather teach them to long for the endless immensity of the sea."
Antoine de Saint-Exupery

1

Understanding Your Organization

"Understand the culture to understand the organization."
Edgar Schein

We all live and work in a complex world made up of complex systems. Everyday we and those around us choose to act in certain ways, and our behavior creates recognizable patterns. These patterns – emerging from the actions, connections and relationships that have meaning across space and time – create culture.

In defining culture, we say that it is the personality of a community, organization or group. It is comprised of the assumptions, values, norms and artifacts of its members and their behaviors. At times culture may be difficult to express, but everyone knows it when they see it and sense it. You can tell the culture of an organization by looking at how the furniture is arranged, what folks brag about, how people are dressed and the rituals that are maintained.

Culture is learned and it provides a reinforcing template shaping what we do and how we think. With this in mind, we have a responsibility to examine and question these templates, keeping an eye out for three potential traps. These are: *"isms," Social Construction* and *Cultural Programming*. All can color our assumptions and alter our perceptions.

We look around and see isms wherever we go. They are doctrine, ideology or theories that categorize individuals and groups. Isms are based upon human qualities that are often different from our own and outside the groups to which we belong; they are, however, present in others. Isms such as racism, ageism or any otherism are sustained by inference, belief, bias, generalizations, habit, ignorance, simplification, stereotypes and tradition. Isms often create particular, unrealistic or negative expectations. For example, when Carol went car shopping, her brother, Teddy, tagged along. The salesman was told Carol was the buyer, but kept addressing himself to Teddy, even to the point of asking, "What color car is she looking for?"

Social construction creates a standard or defines a principle believed to be fact that has been developed or "constructed" through social practice. This *truth* appears to be natural, or the way things are, but can, in fact, be based simply upon history, repetition or habit. For example, a woman is not (educated, intelligent, strong, agile, tough) enough to be a (commander, cardiac surgeon, electrician, financial analyst, CEO).

Finally, there is cultural programming. Because of what we "know," either implicitly or explicitly, we do not just observe a behavior, event or situation; we also attach meaning to it and then act based upon that meaning. Our interpretation of an action or interaction therefore includes an evaluative or judgmental component. The danger lies in the potential for *mis*interpretation. For example, you are from a different part of the country than I. The first time we meet, I make a rash of judgments about you based exclusively on where you were born and your accent.

Notwithstanding these hazards, there is good news here. Complex adaptive systems are collections of individuals who act in a variety of predictable and unpredictable ways and whose actions are interconnected. We are all members of these organizations, communities and other systems. Our actions create the potential to make a difference and with each and every movement, we can transform the system.

The tools we need are simple: looking inside ourselves for self-awareness and self-acknowledgement; conscious reflection that leads to action and resolve; and reaching out to others in cooperation and collaboration. Those, in combination with respect, fairness and balance, will allow us to act. That is, to do our jobs – to facilitate, motivate, negotiate, initiate, communicate, mitigate, innovate, and lead – and to do it well.

The Nature of Complex Adaptive Systems

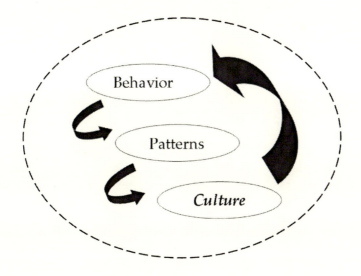

Remember, we have the power to *influence* the systems of which we are part – *and alter the culture.*

What is the culture you would like to create in your organization?

2
Defining Leadership

> *"First say to yourself what you would be;*
> *and then do what you have to do."*
> Epictetus

There is a wide body of literature that explores and expounds on the nature of leadership. These include an array of social, political, professional and personal contexts, and each of us can name numerous famous, as well as infamous, examples. Within every definition of leadership – whether you ascribe to the "learned" or "born with" school of thought – are common denominators. We can easily list those, too.

To me, leadership is personal: not only how I choose to describe and model those qualities and feats, but also what is important to me. It is not enough to say a leader provides vision and purpose; what does that mean for those around her? The parameters for leadership always include the implications for others.

Not too long ago, during a time of transition, I brought a group of senior managers together to talk about leadership. The corporate officers were asked to identify what leadership meant to them, particularly in terms of managing their organization.

The following is a broad list of what the group came up with.

- Provides vision and purpose
- Maintains visibility
- Is comfortable asking for help
- Shares control and authority
- Sets high standards and expectations
- Recognizes and honors the achievements of others
- Invests in people and supports staff with kindness, respect and fairness
- Sets a good example
- Has the right people by his or her side
- Creates the organizational culture
- Makes decisions
- Pursues ongoing learning and growth, challenging people to stretch
- Pulls people together
- Communicates effectively
- Demonstrates passion and dedication
- Recognizes and understands the big picture
- Exemplifies responsibility, accountability, honesty and personal integrity
- Contributes to corporate growth, success and the accomplishment of excellence

It is a long and impressive list. Each characteristic is worthy of being an aspiration, complementing and supplementing the others. I know which are the most important to me.

But before you decide on the most significant for you, think about the following. What "contains" your image of leadership? What characterizes the difference that makes a difference to you in being a leader? What do you believe is

Vision Driven

critical in your connections to others for leading? Lastly, what patterns do you see and what then emerges for you from you own life experiences and reflection when you think about strength and vision?

Now you are ready.

If you had to select the five leadership characteristics that you believe are the most important, which would they be?

3

Strategic Planning

> *"If one does not know to which port one is sailing, no wind is favorable."*
> Seneca

Strategic Planning is a management tool, period. As with any management tool, strategic planning is used with purpose and that is to help an organization do a better job. It allows an organization and its leaders to focus their energy, to ensure that members of the organization are working toward the same goals and to assess and adjust the organization's direction in response to a dynamic and complex environment.

Management needs to be prepared to respond rapidly to the ever-changing landscape. Efficiencies, flexibility and benchmarking are part of the new set of rules. With effective planning you can create a framework for strategic management and thinking as you continually ask the question, "Are we doing the right thing?" This entails attention to *the big picture* and the willingness to adapt to changing circumstances. It consists of the following elements.

- Setting goals and developing an approach to achieving those goals
- Maintaining the clarity and discipline to be productive

- Paying attention to shifting and emerging patterns of behavior and corporate culture
- Making fundamental decisions and choices about what to do, why and how to do it, and then acting
- Shaping and guiding an organization, using resources successfully and focusing on the future

Strategic planning should be a balance between theory and practice, offering you the ability to translate gains in operations and function into sustainable, long-term competitive advantage and value. Recognize that this is a dynamic process and not a one-shot deal. Maintain a solid pace of activity and ensure that staff at every level are informed and involved in providing input. As trust develops, the planning process will help shift the culture in the organization. It goes without saying that management and board commitment must be secured upfront to follow up and follow through on the plans that are created.

Finally, create a balanced scorecard for identifying critical success factors. Specify action steps, outcome measures and accountabilities to track your success.

So, what is planning?

Planning is a comprehensive process that includes setting goals, developing plans and related activities. Planning allows you to reduce uncertainty and facilitate the anticipation and acceptance of change. We create a framework for managerial objectives, opening up multi-directional and multi-tiered communication and setting the stage for smart decision making.

There are other points to consider. Planning also allows

Vision Driven

you to engage in planned change versus reactive change. Planned change is designed and implemented in an orderly and timely fashion in anticipation of future events. Think about succession planning, business-continuity planning and risk-management planning and start with possible or probable scenarios, such as the CEO will be retiring in two years. These types of planning allow organizations to prepare to meet the challenges and opportunities that the coming and anticipated change may present.

Reactive change, on the other hand, is a piecemeal response to circumstances as they develop. For example, a hurricane has shut down the southeastern office for an indeterminate period of time. Reactive response: *Now what do we do?*

Planning is also futuristic. It begins in the future and works its way backward toward the present. Whether you are writing a project proposal, planning an office move or celebrating a significant milestone in the life of your organization, you start with the completion or due date and work your way back through the time between then and now. Identify the tasks that need to be accomplished and how you are going to accomplish them.

Finally, your strategic planning process begins with some very basic questions.

- Based upon your assessments of what you know and what you need to do, how do you move forward as an organization, maintaining value for your customers?
- What is the structure and culture that will support

what you need to do?
- How are you going to ensure that you are effectively executing your plan?

How do you answer these questions for yourself and your organization?

4
Developing the Management Team

"Teams are collections of people who must rely on group collaboration if each member is to experience optimum success and goal achievement."
William Dyer

No one individual ever has the entire combination of experience, skills and talent that a finely tuned management team can have. Each individual brings his or her own diverse background and perspective to the organizational table working toward a common goal. Management wants to develop and promote an ongoing process that strengthens the ability of the group to provide shared leadership. As a CEO, my goal, for this veteran, talented cohort, is for them to integrate in a way that would create a critical level of quality.

The relationship among team members to each other and the CEO is a critical piece of achieving corporate success. It is essential for there to be trust among team members; for their overall effectiveness, both individually and collectively, to be optimal; for their ability to think strategically and act tactically to be expanded; and for accountability to be enhanced.

Begin with Expectations.

I believe in expectations. A leader should work hard to make sure that expectations are clearly stated and support the vision. If you can articulate thoughts and ideas consistently and with as much precision as possible, you can greatly reduce ambiguity, as well as the potential for misinterpretation and error.

People need to know what the expectations are. Clarify and communicate exactly how you define the spectrum of results, from successful to unacceptable. This includes what matters to your organization.

Next, in order to get the job done what resources do you need? As a manager and supervisor, I always ask, "What can I do to help? What do you need from me? What resources can I provide or secure for you in the way of information, training, contacts or time?"

I listen carefully to the answers I get to these questions. Sometimes folks will go off and accomplish what they need to on their own; sometimes they require more time and direction. If I don't know which they need, I cannot be effectively supportive as their leader and then someone may potentially fail. Therefore, we always need to pay attention and be prepared to take our lead from others.

Finally, what are the consequences, implications, benefits and/or rewards of meeting those expectations or not meeting them? This invariably needs to be part of the conversation. I strongly believe it is in everyone's best interest – particularly the organization's – to hold people accountable.

The expectation for managers is simple: Leadership. You

Vision Driven

want them to step up to the plate, be there for each other and be there for the organization.

Of course the reality is that no matter what the boss says or does or how responsibility and authority are delegated, it is both implicit and explicit that s/he owns 50.01 percent of the leadership stock. This means s/he is in charge. But that still leaves plenty of room for others to lead. Once again, in order for this partnership to be successful, you have to articulate and clarify your expectations for each other.

Ask each other and answer for each other the following questions:

- *What does the team want, need or expect from the CEO?*
- *What does the CEO think the team wants, needs or expects from him/her?*
- *What does the CEO want, need or expect from the team?*
- *What does the team think the CEO wants, needs or expects from them?*
- *What does the CEO appreciate about the team and see as their contributions?*
- *What does the team appreciate about the CEO and see as his/her contributions?*
- *What does the team want the CEO to start, stop or continue doing?*
- *What does the CEO want the team to start, stop, or continue doing?*

When you are finished, carefully examine your responses together. What are the similarities? What are the differences? Where are there gaps? How will you bridge them?

As officers of an organization, senior managers are, of course, held to a higher standard. From a global perspective their responsibilities may include:

- Preparing, organizing and controlling activities of the corporation
- Understanding operations
- Strategic thinking and planning
- Policies and procedures
- Financial management
- Business development and marketing
- Appreciating the sense of urgency in their work

However, on the ground, these leadership criteria can be sorted into the following containers.

Communication: The team's thoughts and ideas, both individually and collectively, are presented in an unambiguous, organized and articulate manner. As leaders they communicate well with others; their skills are excellent and they can represent the company in a straightforward and consistent manner. They are sensitive to the impact on the listener and adjust their styles as appropriate.

Alliance-building: Leaders build alliances within and among units as needed to achieve high performance on the stated objectives. They encourage collaboration and teamwork, actively contributing to cohesiveness and cooperation among associates. As team players, they are concerned with the entire organization and their cooperative spirit extends beyond their immediate units or departments. They deal with others effectively to encourage them to build and sustain alliances.

Problem-solving: Leaders consistently demonstrate insight in analyzing problems, determining practical solutions and effectively implementing decisions. They carefully consider consequences; after recognizing a problem, they make timely, practical and cost-effective decisions.

Planning: Leaders set appropriate goals and priorities while consistently defining accountabilities and the work at hand. They anticipate change and arrange work activities to achieve results.

Initiative/Innovation: Leaders are self-starters, willing and able to take independent action. They demonstrate original thinking, ingenuity and creativity in developing new or improved methods and procedures. They routinely exert extra effort in getting the job done while pursuing acceptance of new ideas and anticipating solutions to emerging situations.

Global Perspective: Leaders maintain a big-picture perspective for the organization, accepting their functional role from a corporate stance.

Employee Relations: Leaders foster a productive working environment, taking steps to promote the appropriate participation, development and maximum utilization of all employees. They also deal with employee concerns effectively.

What steps can you take to strengthen your own leadership team?

5

Managing Change

"It is not necessary to change. Survival is not mandatory."
                    W. Edwards Deming

This we know: Change is an unavoidable fact of life, and even in the best of circumstances, it can be difficult. Individuals and organizations worldwide are confronting more turbulent markets, more demanding shareholders and more discerning customers. They are all scrambling to meet the challenges of the day. In every aspect of our lives - personal, professional and in our environment - each one of us faces both wanted and unwanted changes.

That is what transitions are all about. Change is defined as an external event or situation, whereas transition is the total reorientation that happens within us. How will you meet the challenge? What are the tools and skills you have to weather the potential storms and find safe harbor? Are you prepared?

According to Dr. William Bridges, one of the foremost thinkers and authors in the areas of change management and personal transition, our feelings about change are the result of our approach to managing (and enjoying!) the journey from here to there, rather than from announcing the destination. Initially we may respond to change with confusion, questions, doubts and a loss of identity. Soon, though, our transition moves from denial and resistance to exploration of the possibilities and finally we progress to commitment.

While we may not be able to control the change around us, we have significant power over how we travel through it.

Think about a significant change you have weathered.

- *Was it planned or unexpected?*
- *What was your role in the change process?*
- *What was within your control and/or sphere of influence?*
- *How did you feel before, during and after the transition?*
- *And now ...?*

All systems, including businesses and organizations, follow a lifecycle that allows for birth, maturity, creative destruction (change!) and renewal. Remembering that change is both implicit and explicit and allows for growth and development helps us to focus on the positive and maintain our resiliency.

Think about your organization today. What has changed since you joined the company? What is the same?

6

The Three B's of Quality

"Quality means doing it right when no one is looking."
Henry Ford

If we mean what we say about quality products and services, we need a framework by which to judge our actions and activities, projects and processes. I created the idea of the "Three B's" as a user-friendly model to do just that.

- You start with a **Baseline**. This means documenting the present state of the process or product, including current performance, productivity and process levels. Where are you right now? Collect, store, and analyze that data or situation.

- Next you seek out and identify **Benchmarks,** those standard measurements against which similar businesses, products, processes or systems are judged. Continually monitor your performance against the organizations that are recognized as "world class" achievers. Where do you stand or fall? Recognize how and why those benchmarks were identified. What would "world class" productivity look like in your organization?

- Finally, you aspire to **Best Practices.** Your goal is to adopt and create practices that demonstrably reduce defects or costs or improve efficiency to a higher level of results. More importantly, you wow your customers and achieve a level of competence and capacity at the highest level. This is where you want to be. Imagine your customer and employee attitudes and actions when you are here.

This all sounds fine but how do you help your staff take their first step in understanding the "wheres and hows" of the process? By focusing on quality, try engaging everyone in a simple brainstorm that brings concepts home to the group.

What are the elements of a quality marriage?

Communication	Diplomacy
Sharing the work	Shared goals and values
Friendship	Compromise
Autonomy	Wisdom
Resources	Love
Laughter	Sharing money
Trust	Sex
Respect	Monogamy
Listening	Show me how
Humor	Acceptance
Commitment	Contentment

If these are your standards or benchmarks, it is up to each individual (significant other) in the organization (relationship) not only to stop and assess their own situations (creating a baseline), but to benchmark where they fall within the whole spectrum of possibilities (percentage of happily married couples with like criteria) and set their sights on the best practice (celebrating a joyous Diamond Wedding Anniversary surrounded by generations of family and friends). Now, just imagine if your starting point is the best practice.

What would your own 3-B framework look like for home or for work?

7

Thinking about the Future

> *"When men speak of the future, the Gods laugh."*
> Chinese Proverb

Part of being human is our desire to predict and control the future. As we become more intelligent and as technology advances, we are constantly learning a thing or two about how much influence we really do have on future events. Forget about psychics and crystal balls; nowadays computer simulations and algorithms present us with sophisticated options for thinking about the future. Of course, there are no guarantees.

In order to shape a preferred future you need to have a picture in your mind of what it is you really want.

Let's take a page from futurists, seers and planners. Imagine it is ten years from now. Think about how old you will be. How old will your children be? How old will your closest friend be? Now let that thought grow.

- What kind of work will you be doing?
- What will you be learning and how will you be learning?
- What will you believe in?
- In what different ways will you find joy?
- What will worry you the most?

- What will you hope for?

Now think about your organization. Remember it is still ten years from now.

- Will it still exist?
- Will it be different? How?
- What will your world of work be like?
- What are your hopes for the future of your company?
- What are the implications for your thinking, planning and actions starting today?

As your challenges become more apparent, you can become more conscious about the gap between the way the world is and the way you would like it to be. You can address this with action.

From a *financial* perspective, this might mean developing new customers and new contracts; better financial and budget management techniques; new operating and accounting systems; and a healthy bottom line.

From a *customer* perspective, this might mean providing and adding value through enhanced relationships; collecting and analyzing client data; developing ground-breaking products and services; shifting to a more innovative culture of doing business; and managing private and public market segmentation.

From a perspective of *organizational excellence*, this might mean expanded, efficient systems, processes and quality standards; an effective communication plan; and enhanced performance management procedures with built in rewards and recognition.

From a perspective of *innovation, learning and creativity,* this might mean escalating research and development functions; expanding the corporate white space; and proactively developing new products and services to remain at the edge of anticipated changing markets.

Individually, you can ask yourself if what you are doing is ...

- Moving you forward to reach your goals?
- Bringing business in the door?

Collectively as a group, your organization can identify what you will need to reach your shared vision.

- Communicating openly, consistently, often and in all directions
- Innovating
- Identifying and measuring internal and external results
- Understanding and responding to your market
- Striving for and achieving excellence
- Maximizing financial and human resources
- Maintaining ongoing dialogues with colleagues and providing resources for improvement
- Showing an appreciation for diversity
- Providing feedback into the system

Keeping this in mind, the following questions are for your careful consideration:

- How will you manage the certainty of uncertainty?
- What are the implications of your answers to these questions in your thinking, planning and actions today?

Now, what are you waiting for?

8
Measuring Results: The Balanced Scorecard

"If we did all the things we were capable of doing, we would literally astound ourselves."
Thomas Edison

Critical success factors are the measures that determine whether or not your organization is successful in achieving its goals. They provide macro containers for organizing and evaluating the outcomes and impacts of your efforts. Through the use of the balanced scorecard, management can distill those key factors that have to be achieved for an organization to be able to realize successful outcomes.

The balanced scorecard, a management system developed by Harvard University's Robert S. Kaplan and David P. Norton, enables organizations to clarify their vision and strategy and translate them into action. It provides feedback around both the internal business processes and external outcomes in order to continuously improve strategic performance and results. I am a huge fan of the balanced scorecard because it focuses efforts on strategy and vision while offering a set of unmistakable measures that give organizations a quick, but comprehensive, view of what is going on.

The scorecard is organized into four key perspectives: *fi-*

nancial perspective, or how to we look to our shareholders, constituents, or funders; *internal business perspective*, or how we have maintained excellence in our business processes and procedures; *customer perspective*, or how our customers see us; and *innovation and learning perspective*, or how we can continue to improve and create value for all our stakeholders. Each point of view can be further interpreted as those specific factors that make sense for an individual organization.

For example, if you specifically identified financial growth and sustainability as a key perspective, one of your critical success factors might be profitability. Your measurement of this might be changes in top-line revenue with respect to the bottom line; analyzing pricing formulas; and whether you are in the red or the black on your financial statements at the end of the year. With quality systems in place – a critical success factor for operational excellence – you would also be able to measure, analyze and project a financial return on investment while tracking smart sustainable growth.

Once you know what your critical success factors are, you can then identify possible measures of your goals and results. Continuing to distill the process, you would then be able to list specific objectives and actions to achieve them.

The following example might be your own organization's scorecard.

Organizational Balanced Scorecard

Key Perspective	Critical Success Factor	Potential Measures
Financial Growth and Sustainability	Growth	Managed growth in top line revenue, increased market share
	Profitability	Healthy bottom line, effective pricing models
	Customer Retention	Percentage of contract renewals
	Increased Share of Wallet	Expansion of business, up-selling to current customers
Delivering Value to Customers	Time	On-time or sooner delivery, as defined by customer
	Quality	Defect- and error free, at a minimum
	Performance and Services	Achieving or exceeding outcomes, as defined by customer
	Cost	Value, as defined by customer
Operational Excellence	Quality	Meeting or exceeding standards
	Performance	Meeting or exceeding goals, accessibility and availability for customer service; customer experience management processes
	Core Competencies	Alignment of resources and expertise to corporate goals
	Resource Management	Work load related to internal/external requirements and capacity
	Knowledge Management	Mechanisms/structure for incubating and energizing capabilities; knowledge and development of internal benchmarking
	Communication	Common understanding and awareness of corporate vision, mission, values, strategy and purpose; multiple open channels of communication and feedback loops
	Systems/Infrastructure	Structure, policies and procedures in place providing the ability to do business on a daily basis
Creativity and Innovation	Future-focused	New product and service development, rapid deployment of R&D functions
	Fluid Staff	Demonstration of expanded core competencies and capabilities in enterprise activities; cross-functional expertise and change
	Maintain the Enterprise	Opportunities and structures to support and encourage enterprise activities, creativity and risk-taking

From here your scorecard can be further expanded. Based upon the company scorecard, each business unit would then create its own targets and measures; and from those unit scorecards, individual staff success factors and scorecards would then filter down. This last step is an undeniable way to show how everyone's individual actions support the whole in very real and connected ways.

The individual's scorecard rolls up to the corporate scorecard; the corporate scorecard rolls down to the individual. You can now answer questions about how you (individually or corporately) are doing and you can see how any one action contributes to the whole.

The bottom line: if the organization is doing well, the individual, such as an employee or customer, is doing well; and if the individual is doing well, the organization is doing well, too.

How well are you performing up and down your organization? How do you know?

9
Smile!

> *"The mind, once expanded to the dimensions of larger ideas, never returns to its original size."*
> Oliver W. Holmes

A very talented colleague of mine, Grace, works for an organization whose value statement is expressed simply as SMILE! They mean it. SMILE is an acronym that stands for: Sincerity, Motivation, Integrity, Laughter and Enthusiasm. I admit I cannot recall meeting anyone recently whose disposition and demeanor were not improved by a smile; however this sounded a bit too good to be true to me.

Grace arranged a meeting for me with the company's Director of Operations. I asked the obvious questions and was assured that *smiling* was indeed standard operating procedure - everyone truly "Smiled." This unique and upbeat environment was the result of a corporate-wide attitude and focus on the positive, rather than negative. "Every company has areas for improvement and deficits that need to be addressed swiftly and in real time," she told me, "including ours. However, this organization has made and carried out a commitment, from the top down, to put their principal energy and support into our assets, strengths and capabilities." Of course she smiled.

This paradigm is akin to Appreciative Inquiry (AI), a theory and practice which seeks out the best in people, organizations and the world at large. An AI approach allows you to center on the positive aspects of any situation through the use of affirming questions. You can then expand that frame of reference to address the negative.

Please note that I am not doing AI justice here – barely scratching the surface of its possibilities. I did, though, like the notion of exploring and then leveraging what was right in a given situation rather than getting stuck on what was wrong.

I decided to try this at "home" at an all-hands meeting. The task was:

Think back on a time at work when you were functioning in a way that made you feel totally alive, completely energized with where you were and what you were doing and able to produce your best work. Who were you with, what were you doing and what did that mean to you at the time? Now, look at your answers; what do you see?

The following themes emerged during the debriefing session:

- Excitement: we were part of a new corporate direction, contributing members of a team, cohesive, trusting and committed
- Excellence: in the midst of chaos we were connected to each other and clients, envisioning the possibilities, doing our best work, united in our task
- Coherence and connection: all barriers were down, everyone was involved and felt needed, valued, ap-

Vision Driven

preciated, unified

- "Wicked good" work from all staff: we were purposeful and directed, with new emerging opportunities and learning
- Appreciation of each other: we valued our differences in thought and contributions
- Celebration: of the results as one whole entity

Try this at your next staff meeting. You will discover that within your own list of themes will be the not-so-secret roadmap to achieving and maintaining employee enthusiasm and drive in your workplace.

The next step is to begin to build these lessons into your everyday work processes. For example, you can potentially achieve cohesion, appreciation and excellence if the ground rules for your next systems update stipulate that no one individual will receive the credit, but the group as a whole will reap the kudos and the rewards.

No doubt you will bump up against barriers. Your task then is to identify an action or strategy to overcome these hurdles. Be sure to challenge yourself to practice diligently each time to jump higher and farther to reach your goal.

Think back on a time at work when you were functioning in a way that made you feel totally alive, completely energized with where you were and what you were doing, and able to produce your best work. Who were you with, what were you doing and what did that mean to you at the time? Now, look at your answers; what do you see?

10

Customer Experience Management

"If you don't take care of your customers, someone else will."
Commonly stated by corporate sales trainers.

I say it with tongue in cheek that every business at some point comes to realize that their main focus must be to satisfy their customers. This goes for manufacturing companies, the service industry, retail stores, non-profit organizations and government agencies, as well as everyone in each of their divisions, departments and branch offices. Customer service is beyond policies and procedures: it is about what takes place during interactions with customers. For example, imagine a situation where you are the customer. How courteous was the sales person in answering your questions? How long did it take for someone to answer the phone or were you put on hold indefinitely? It may also refer to the identifiable, but sometimes intangible, activities undertaken by a company in conjunction with the basic goods and services it sells.

The elements of good customer service are not hard to determine. A simple brainstorm with a corporate sales team came up with the following list of quality factors:

- Meeting/exceeding someone's needs, going above and beyond
- Building trust and rapport

- Paying attention
- Defusing the stress or anger in a situation
- Identifying the real issues
- Anticipating, being proactive
- Having an investment in the outcome and the relationship
- Putting yourself in someone else's place
- Following-up/following-through
- Doing what you say you are going to do
- Coming to a successful resolution

Beyond the immediate outcomes of an exchange between organizations and clients, is the concept of the total customer experience. This speaks to the overall impression of the product based on the client's exchanges and experiences with people, products, services and solutions in acquiring and using that product. Organizations need to manage that customer experience carefully.

Customer experience management, or CEM, has been defined as "the process of strategically managing a customer's entire experience with a product or a company." CEM highlights the notion that beyond the sale organizations need to truly understand what it means to create value for their customers, as well as an excellent customer experience.

This requires the following.

- Understanding best practices and the practices of your competition
- Developing a comprehensive approach to solutions
- Delivering high value to the customer

- Producing internal consistency across the corporation
- Meeting customer expectations for both processes and outcomes
- Offering flexibility of products and services to respond to clients' needs

CEM includes three steps. The first is discovering the clients' expectations. What do they have in mind and what is their desired outcome? The second is shaping services and products to meet client expectations. After all, the customer is always right. The third is making sure the customer is satisfied. Has the product or service met client expectations and how do you know?

For customer experience management to be effective, your approach must be comprehensive.

- Adapting to the needs of various projects and clients
- Covering all client contact from the first call to the final meeting
- Allowing the organization to learn how to improve products and services
- Using consistent corporate-wide tools for measuring client satisfaction, such as account management satisfaction surveys
- Including standard ways to respond to customer complaints or concerns, such as protocol, an escalation process and clear documentation of steps
- Allowing staff to evaluate performance against the client's desired outcomes and expectations
- Integrating with processes across the corporation

Clients know what they want when it comes to process and that is excellence. Meeting those expectations means that organizations must find a common ground between total customization for each and every client and the rigid consistency of products and services. For example, are you building each and every computer to your customers' particular specifications and requirements; or are you creating a line of finely-tuned training shoes that are ready off-the-shelf to meet the needs of fitness enthusiasts with varying degrees of skill and form?

Alternately, clients may not know about their intended outcomes and opportunities. Therefore, it is your role to provide support through trend analysis, use of competitive intelligence, asking good questions and being open to radical inquiry. For example, your customer is far from home and an emergency situation erupts. Is your answer, "Of course we'll take care of it," or "We're not allowed to do that?"

Corporate staff needs to know *what* the important *it* is, *how* to do it, and *whether* or not they are meeting customer expectations. As a customer-oriented organization your targets should be obvious.

- Adding customer value
- Focusing on results
- Seeing the bigger picture (the big *it*)
- Educating the customer and expanding their view
- Developing consulting relationships with clients
- Building and maintaining credibility
- Opening the door to finding out about the client's world

- Asking questions
- Using an inquiry stance

Think also about your own desired outcomes for your customer interactions. Anyone can be a vendor; your aspiration, however, is to partner with your clients for mutual benefit and satisfaction.

Ultimately, the goal is to raise the quality of service you are providing in order to enhance and manage the customer's experience. Think about the last time you had a question or problem with a product or service. What were you hoping for? Well that is the resolution you want to be for your customers. Even if you do not make the sale, your customer can walk away without that pair of cross-trainers but with a positive experience they will remember, talk about, recommend to others and lead them to return another day.

Finally, remember your critical internal customers as well: the folks who work with you and beside you every day. This is, after all, your team we are talking about. Your efforts here are no less essential so be sure to include an abundance of respect, fairness and appreciation.

What actions or changes does your organization need to make in response to customer expectations and feedback for maintaining an overall excellent customer experience?

11
Managers as Leaders

"Leaders grow; they are not made."
Peter Drucker

Dear Senior Team:

As a group of individuals who have the day-to-day responsibilities of managing a corporation, you have the honor and the responsibility to be consistently participating or otherwise involved in what is going on around you. On the one hand, your roles are defined. On the other hand, they also continue to emerge and be redefined as circumstances dictate. Gleaned from the extensive body of business literature, my own random thoughts on leadership go something like this.

Leaders are people who:

- Lead as well as manage
- Motivate and set an example for others in all that they do
- Know what they are responsible for and do it
- Recognize and understand the big picture
- Exemplify personal integrity, respect and fairness
- Participate in defining and implementing corporate strategy
- Support staff at every turn

- Participate in corporate growth, success and the accomplishment of excellence

My expectations for you as a group are that you will:

- Do the job
- Learn the business
- Pay attention
- Lead by example
- Be strategically in sync with organizational goals and each other
- Stand behind and for the CEO
- Get the best out of each others' brains
- Focus on the customer
- Actively participate
- Carry each others' water
- Push the frontier of our collective thoughts and actions

That is where I would set the bar. I know you are up to the task!

Thank you,

Mallary

What do your managers need to hear from you?

12

Preparing for the Unknown

> *"Trying to predict the future is like trying to drive down a country road at night with no lights while looking out the back window."*
> Peter Drucker

We learn to deal with change however it comes. When crises occur, we face a new paradigm. In the midst of upheaval to the system, there is an event or turning point in the evolution of the organization. The organization may recover and continue along a generally desirable path, or the organization may suffer a serious decline in capabilities and performance – perhaps to the point of no return.

As such, according to noted author and business guru Warren Bennis, we must operate with certain assumptions. Crisis cannot be stopped; it is, after all, part of life and part of doing business and the impact can be far reaching. At a minimum there is disruption of normal functioning. This includes a significant loss of focus. Fear and uncertainty are pervasive and values and priorities are questioned. The result is an undeniable desire to retain and sustain a degree of normalcy. The most important piece, however, is maintaining business continuity.

A crisis-mitigation process gives you options for action and ways to understand what needs to be done. Where is the organization right now and where does it need to go? Working with your entire team, you must divine and then design the future organization, creating the strategy, plans and materials to get you there. Then, do it! Execute your plan, monitor progress at all levels and learn together what you need to do to continuously improve the process.

Part of your capacity then as an organization is to develop resiliency, that ability to recover quickly from change or misfortune. Your keys to success are:

- Confident leadership
- Strategic planning
- Smooth coordination
- Eager cooperation
- Open communication
- Competent execution
- A pinch of luck

Start by returning to and relying on your foundation: your mission, values, culture, diversity, quality and balance. Next, take advantage of your leadership strengths. Believe in the possible, approach others with unconditional positive regard, support an honest ongoing conversation, pay attention and be able to be counted on.

Your actions should reflect your experience and expertise, as well as your resiliency.

- Look to the long-term horizon
- Focus on hopes and dreams
- Think best-case scenario

- Seek, recognize and honor small acts of kindness
- Apply lessons learned
- Provide opportunities for work as a source of community and meaning in people's lives
- Work to develop and maintain competence, confidence and capacity throughout your organization

Be sure to reinforce decisions and actions that are internally consistent with other parts of the organization and stop those that are not. In addition, recognize each person's contribution to the planning process and what may be at risk for the organization.

Your mantra should state: "If it can happen, it probably will." Not everything happens according to the plan. Nothing ever stays the same, either, so preparedness is a continuous process. Involve as many of your team members as possible in the opportunity to go beyond and make a difference.

Sometimes you only get one chance to do it right. Take the time and energy to build personal relationships in order to work and play well with others. As we've all learned working and playing well with others takes practice.

So, if your organization doesn't work well now ...?

13

A Framework for Action

"When you think a fastball is coming you gotta be ready to hit the curve."
Jaja Q.

Policy establishes corporate-wide expectations for process, products, services and action.

Procedure establishes disciplined ways to define and deliver products and services.

Decisions are made with attention to data, history, context and corporate-wide policies and procedures.

Action is taken in consonance with the established decisions, procedures and policy and pursued within this framework with optimal individual accountability.

What is the fastball that is coming at you?

14
What Matters Most

"Let's make a dent in the universe."
Steve Jobs

There has been a dramatic shift in priorities in the workplace, wherever the workplace is. The dichotomy between personal values and professional life no longer exists. In every facet of life, people are focusing more and more on what matters most.

According to workplace studies conducted across the country, when employees are asked what motivates them and sustains their energy and enthusiasm, it is less likely to be about salary and benefits and more likely to be about quality of work life and meaningful work. This is consistent with years of research in the social sciences that have identified a handful of basic human requirements that must be present for people to be motivated and productive. The following criteria provide a foundation for designing an effective organization and a healthy workplace.

- The ability to make decisions
- Opportunities to learn on the job and to continue learning
- Variety and challenges in tasks and responsibilities
- Mutual support, appreciation, respect and fairness
- A path for ongoing personal and professional

growth and development
- Meaningfulness and being able to make the connection between daily work and the broader social context

It takes effort to create this workplace, where people are proud and pleased to say they belong. However, the opportunity to be a part of this new, more inclusive, integrative and flexible community does not come easily. It happens through individual and joint effort and high levels of participation or sweat equity. It is dependent on a collective state of mind, strong relationships among members, a high level of trust, a clear commitment, leadership throughout the ranks and an understanding that "we are the organization."

It means answering the following tough questions.

- How can you create an environment that enables each person to reach his or her potential?
- How is the creation of value in your organization maximized while respecting the needs of each person in it?
- How is success measured for both the individual and the organization?
- Is respect and dignity for everyone inside and outside your organization part of business as usual?
- Are your mission and values interdependent as well as independent and consistent with what you do?
- What are you truly contributing to the big picture?

Recently, a colleague generously shared with me an e-mail she received from her brother who was soon to return home from Iraq. In it he said, "I feel very fortunate to have had the honor to take part in an event that will shape the history of the world and have such a significant impact on generations to come. I hope when scholars and politicians look back on it, they do so to acknowledge our efforts to make the world a better place. It is an honor to serve our nation and to be able to serve with so many fine men and women."

This is not a political statement, but rather an individual acknowledgement that each of us strives to be part of something that is valuable, is productive and offers us an opportunity to test our mettle. We seek opportunities where getting the job done includes hope and hopefulness, help and helpfulness, meaning and meaningfulness.

It is in this environment that we can achieve balance in body, mind and spirit. It is not just about saving the world but also about creating the means for everyone to be part of an organization or community with confidence and commitment, loyalty and pride. It's *what matters most.*

What are the ways in which you can support and engage your employees in what matters most?

PART II

The Lessons

> *"Being a philosopher, I have a problem for every solution."*
> Robert Zend

15

The Personal Equation

"We don't see things as they are, we see them as we are."
Anaïs Nin

Your personal equation is who you are. It is about your nature and nurture, those things that you have learned to appreciate and value – what is really important to you – as well as your hardwiring. You weigh those factors as you see fit and translate them into the words, actions, thoughts and ideas you have and do everyday. How you are the same and how you are different from others is a simple way to express the equation, in addition to how you want to be, how you act in your personal and professional life and how you relate to others.

Elizabeth Smith in her book *Creating Productive Organizations*, defines personal equation as "... the tendency to personal bias which accounts for the variation in interpretation or approach, and for which allowance must be made." Think about yourself as an array of personal factors and variables connected to both professional and social environments. The equations can include diverse aspects of ourselves, in order of priority or not, and are exemplified by what we do, say and think everyday. For example, I have a colleague who wants to learn something new from each experience. For her, this sets up a model of how she approaches every situation, frames her questions and pays attention to what is going on around her.

How we interpret and operate in the world is a reflection of our personal equations. My personal equation says quite a bit about me, but I like to let people know what they are getting into.

- I ask questions and use a proactive approach.
- Honesty and personal integrity are paramount.
- I count my blessings.
- I look for reasons to laugh and people to laugh with.
- I always expect more from myself and others.
- The big picture is all there is.
- It's worth the risk.

What is your personal equation?

16
Maintaining the Helm

"The time is always right to do what is right."
Martin Luther King Jr.

On September 11, 2001, our organization was situated between New York City and Boston. Even at the distance of one hundred miles, we felt the vibrations of the day's events personally and professionally, like everyone else around the globe.

We did what we needed to do. We checked that our employees who were in New York City for training at the time were alright. We connected with all staff members across the country. We spoke with clients and customers and began marshaling resources for support. We prepared managers and service providers to go out into the field.

I remember feeling sad on so many levels and thinking at the time that I should be going out there with our staff: touching customers, providing support and being a visible presence to our care and commitment, ready to do what I was asking employees to do. Of course, I didn't. My place was in the office along side those troops who stood their posts and did their jobs. I have no claim to extraordinary actions: I simply did my job, being there, steady at the helm.

Many of our staff scattered in response to client needs. For those of us who stayed at home, on Friday, September 14th, I organized a comfort lunch for everyone who could be there. We all wore red, white and blue; ate lots of junk food and sugar; played Pin the Tail on the Donkey, Musical Chairs and other silly games; and we talked. It was a cathartic afternoon for us, creating and protecting a temporary silly space for ourselves to take a breather and recharge our batteries.

Looking back several months later on those events we realized that we learned a thing or two about our work (and ourselves) and so we turned to each other and asked how we could use the experience. We needed to continue to grow the good stuff and learn. We also wanted to amplify the best things and not dampen the energy of individuals towards their work.

Sometimes it is a matter of perceptions. For example, when I said how proud I was of the outstanding work and contributions of everyone in our response to the events of September 11th, someone piped up, "But isn't this what we are supposed to do?" In that moment I thought of how different our viewpoints were and recognized the need to build common ground. So I asked our staff how we could bridge these disparate views; their many responses provided learning for us all.

- Build common expectations about the meaning of success. How close is close enough to count?
- Celebrate and build rituals to reinforce success as it happens.
- Tell stories to focus and support recollection.
- Identify outcomes, then measure actions and results.

Vision Driven

- Talk about what is happening to build shared perceptions.
- See our collective behaviors as a jigsaw puzzle to focus on the parts and on the whole.
- Monitor the process explicitly; when complete, document with after-action reviews.
- Set end dates and review accordingly.
- Build structures to support accountability.
- Document lessons learned so we continue to get better.
- Create an environment where corporate priorities count.
- Focus on the part of an opportunity that remains, rather than on the part we might have missed.
- Frame and reframe objectives.
- Build an early-warning system and be ready to move into action.
- Have the right resources and keep those resources fluid.
- Work on triage together and set priorities.
- Learn, reflect and share.

We all took something important from those tough days and the ones thereafter. Looking back, for me personally and practically, it was both more complex and simple at the same time. When the noise dissipated, one lesson for me was where the leader needed to be and what that vantage point afforded me.

Where are you when the big and little things happen in your organization?

17
Ideas Anyone?

> *"If at first the idea is not absurd, then there is no hope for it."*
> Albert Einstein

Sometimes it seems to take a truly brave person to propose a new, innovative or different idea at work. After all, we've all been there and done that when it comes to stopping ideas cold in their tracks. Raise your hand at each of the following comments that you've heard in the past at meetings or other occasions when people have been asked for their suggestions and given them.

- *"We tried that already and it didn't work."*
- *"Are you serious? Come on ..."*
- *"Are you kidding?"*
- *"They'll never buy that."*
- *"That's not what we had in mind."*
- *"Nice thought. Any other brilliant ideas?"*
- *"I'm not sure you know enough about it."*
- *"You're not suggesting we do that, are you?"*
- *"We'll never make it work."*
- *"It won't last."*
- *"It'll cost too much."*
- *"Can't we be logical?"*
- *"Yes, but ... "*

Enough said. The only thing missing is the accompanying "tsk" and roll of the eyes. How do you think the people who were offering their ideas felt? How did you feel?

Part of your responsibilities, whether as an employer or employee, is to help promote and ensure an organizational environment of openness and trust, especially when it comes to new ideas. Of course, there are the possibilities for new and exciting opportunities and return on investment. But think about this, too: if ideas are heard with an open mind and treated with reason and respect, everyone will be more engaged and productive, sharing their insights, views and brainstorms.

Speaking of which, when you are feeling stuck or fresh out of ideas one of the fastest and easiest ways to get unstuck is also one of my favorite tools, a simple brainstorm. It's a technique we are all familiar with. Don't underestimate the value of thinking out loud together.

Start with identifying the problem or situation, then ask for random, free-flowing responses from your team. The purpose here is to conceive original, wide-ranging and even absurd ideas that can lead to viable solutions.

The basic rules for brainstorming are:

- All ideas are captured.
- There are no wrong answers or dumb ideas.
- Everything gets written down (to be considered later).
- This is a non-judgmental process; you are simply collecting peoples' thoughts and input.
- Everyone participates.

- Be as creative, open and perhaps wild as possible.
- Get as many responses as you can.

After the brainstorming is complete there is an open discussion among the group, considering all the ideas listed. Some may be expanded, some grouped together or collapsed into each other. This process continues until there is a practical list of alternatives to weigh.

This is only the beginning of seeing that idea through to fruition. There is still plenty of work to be done. However, remember that whatever solution or path you decide to pursue, your team is already invested in it. After all, they have contributed to the creative process from the beginning.

Good work!

Where does your organization need a good brainstorm?

18

The Whole Package

> *"He was the one employee we all knew: bright, funny, charismatic. Could always make me laugh. We loved to go out to lunch with him but no one wanted to work with him. Simply could not be counted on."*
> One former colleague talking about another

When the going gets tough, you may wonder if you have the best people in your organization to manage the work and do the job that needs to be done. Jim Collins wrote thoughtfully about getting the right people on the bus and putting them in the right seats. There are many concrete ways to measure whether someone is performing the tasks assigned or meeting the sales targets in their quarterly goals. Based on research, as well as hands-on experience, I use three criteria to set the bar.

<u>Ability</u>: What are the skills, aptitudes, talents, knowledge, experience and expertise essential to accomplish the task, and does the individual meet those requirements? In other words, *Can he do he job?*

<u>Motivation</u>: Given the choices at hand and the consequences of action, is there commitment to see the task through? In other words, *Will he do the job?*

<u>Accountability</u>: Once the task is done, is there the neces-

sary follow up that deals with potential next steps and implications for the whole? In other words, *Does he successfully conclude the job?*

Once you begin to weigh these factors against your staff assets, you may find yourself bumping smartly into the same obstacle I did: the notion of the whole package. Each individual is, of course, a composite of a variety of strengths and weaknesses, talents and faults, competence and incompetence, at varying degrees. This is where it becomes tricky.

A colleague of mine shared an experience that was part of a reorganization process at her company. Management was tasked to make a determination about whether or not to keep a particular individual. On the plus side, this was a long-time employee who was fully acquainted with the business and business processes, knew all the customers and was well liked and trusted by the clients. She was the queen of customer service. She put in whatever hours it took to get the job done, had a strong commitment to the work and was capable of thinking on a highly conceptual level for planning and strategy. She also had a quirky sense of humor which charmed most people she met.

On the flip side she was completely disorganized and overwhelmed by details and paperwork. Her desk and office were a whirlwind. Contract documents were consistently late. She barely managed the administrative pieces of her job and she had difficulty maintaining personal and professional boundaries.

The bottom line was that what she did well, she did exceptionally well; there was no equal. Where she lacked skills and discipline, she slowed the rest of the team and caused bottle-necks throughout the organization. My colleague's challenge was to maximize her employee's time doing what she did well, not what she liked doing. While there is a strong correlation between the tasks we do well in the job and the tasks we enjoy doing, the company could not afford to have the employee just do what she liked to do.

As part of an honest discussion and performance appraisal, I suggested giving the employee the following assignment:

Think about what you like to do, what you enjoy doing and what you believe you are particularly skilled at doing. Also think about where you could use some development in skills and competencies. Once those thoughts emerge answer this question: based upon what you know and understand about yourself, what is the ideal position for you and is it here?

The employee was tickled pink with what she was asked to do. She said no one had ever asked her to do anything like that before and she was actually looking forward to sitting down with herself and figuring it out. She was forewarned that there was no guarantee that her ideal job would be waiting when she got done, but the opportunity provided her with a process to clear away some assumptions and misconceptions about the work and herself. The stage was now set for a meaningful dialogue.

Of course, she remained with the company. Working together, she and her supervisor came up with a way to optimize the time she spent on the job and show a return on those things she excelled at, while minimizing or delegating those things that were counter-productive to her success. The company was also wise enough to have administrative support readily available to organize her space, files and her work life to simplify processes for everyone.

It may seem like she was rewarded for not performing all of her assigned responsibilities but that was not the case. There was a significant boost to the employee's self-esteem, energy and enthusiasm. She experienced a renewed level of awareness and appreciation of others and their diversity of skills, talents and commitment to the work. In addition, it was not lost on other staff members that a supervisor's responsibility includes creatively facilitating employee success.

It was worth it for all concerned.

Are you taking advantage of the entire package of those who work with you?

19

The 10-Minute Rule

"The best surprise is no surprise."
Holiday Inn

More than two years before the attacks on the World Trade Center in New York City and the Pentagon in Arlington, Virginia, and with less than 30 days into the job, we had a bomb scare in our building. I had traveled down to New Orleans for a professional association meeting and was scheduled to present research findings as part of a panel. I also had hopes of connecting with a former military colleague. I arrived late Tuesday, planned to return home on Sunday and be back in the office on Monday.

On Friday afternoon I received a voice mail message from one of our senior team members. There had been a bomb threat in the building; everyone was fine, but the office was closed for the rest of the day. Not to worry.

I called him back immediately and got whatever details he had. There had been an anonymous call into the building management office stating that a bomb had been placed in the building and was set to go off. The local police arrived, cleared the premises and began a floor-by-floor search. As part of the search, they asked representatives from each office to go back inside and see if anything obvious was amiss: something there that shouldn't have been or something gone that should have been there. A corporate officer took on the task, did an office sweep and decided that everything looked fine. After repeating this process with all tenants, the police declared the building was safe and people were given permission to return.

What followed on the scene was a lengthy and rather confrontational discussion among our staff about whether it was truly safe to go back inside. The bomb squad would not be finished with their search until the following day, but people were given a choice as to whether or not to return to their offices. It was finally determined that everyone would go home. We'd close and wait for official clearance over the weekend. Frankly, I was greatly relieved that all our folks were out of the building, but I was confused. I asked senior staff members what had been corporate procedure in the past for emergency situations beyond fire drills. There wasn't one. Okay.

I changed my flights and came home on Saturday. On Sunday morning I drove to the office. Police were still there – a very visible presence for a Sunday morning – and so were representatives from building management. I met with them both and was told that the entire building had been swept by the bomb squad and declared clear. Also, after further investigating, it was determined that the threat was the work of a disgruntled former employee of the one of the tenants – not us! – and nothing more than a prank. There never had been a real threat to the building.

I went up to the office and did a quick tour to review the state of things as they had been left on Friday. After catching up and sifting through the piles of paper on my own desk, I left a broadcast voice mail for staff. There would be an all-hands meeting the following morning. Attendance was mandatory.

With three and a half weeks in the job, I recalled that one of the items on my never-ending to-do list was *review emergency and facilities procedures and compliance with staff.* Today that item would have been bumped way up on the list; this was, however, during those semi-innocent days before September 11, 2001, if any of us can remember back that far.

I had previous experience with threat management and assessment. At the time of the terrorist attack at the Alfred P. Murrah Federal Building in Oklahoma City, Oklahoma, on April 19, 1995, I was working with the Department of the Army in Washington, DC. I was familiar with threats, drills, risk assessment, check lists, crisis communications and threat management teams. I also knew what we needed to do now.

On Monday morning we got right down to business. "There's no blame here, except maybe the local authorities for being pretty cavalier with regard to allowing folks back into the building before the bomb squad had been here. I am, however, concerned about how this situation was handled. I want to be sure that we are prepared for next time. I am thinking about Plan B, and I am obviously also talking about events beyond natural catastrophes."

We formed a threat management team with representatives from across all units who would research policies and procedures for small to midsize businesses and resources in the greater Hartford area. The team created a survey for all employees to complete to give us baseline data on perceptions, expectations and realities. They would then develop a draft policy for the company, which would be reviewed, modified as necessary and then implemented.

On a macro level the important considerations were easily identified:

Security: Maslow's laws tell us that if we do not feel safe and secure, growth and maturity are beyond our reach. Therefore, this is critical and the end to be sought.

Integrity: Maintain the internal and external connections between values, thought and deed. This keeps a focus on all sides of a situational equation and hopefully maintains the thread of what is important.

Accountability: With ongoing concentration on the internal and external functions and vulnerabilities, lines of accountability are easier to maintain and monitor – not in an unrealistic or inappropriate way, but to keep top-of-mind as a proactive means of avoiding missteps or mischief.

Relationships: Do not forget the roles and goals of partnerships and other business relationships across all segments and including all levels of responsibility. These, too, are critical connections.

Our plan, like most plans today included the following basics:

- Protect the corporate infrastructure. This means backup and security for all telecommunications hardware and software, systems and energy flows.

- Assess the risks. Where are your vulnerabilities, strengths and challenges? Be proactive and think in terms of what you need to preserve and protect. September 11, 2001 certainly expanded the delta of possibilities of events, so challenge yourself to do some serious worst-case scenario planning.
- Have emergency supplies on hand. This includes a first aid kit, flashlights, radio, water, batteries, blankets and some basic high-protein snacks.
- Do regular backups of data and keep those records and any other significant must-have documentation in a separate, different location. This location should be as accessible as possible.
- Review your insurance policies and be sure you have what you need.
- Know your escape routes. Plan for a possible evacuation, conduct drills and have procedures and check-in points down pat.
- Business continuity planning. Know what you need to keep doing business; be sure you have contact information on personnel and customers and identify alternate ways to communicate, such as through your website.
- Finally, plan for an emergency. Review everyone's roles and responsibilities, know who is in charge of procedures, who is the spokesperson and who will make decisions. Even small organizations, that do not have access to unlimited resources or technology, can create a smart and carefully thought-out plan. The key in any emergency situation is to ensure that everyone is informed and acts smartly and safely.

As CEO, the health and safety of all is your first and most important responsibility. Having said that, however, being CEO means you need to have good information in a timely fashion to make the best decisions. That is what you are paid for. So, after that first incident, I implemented *The 10-Minute Rule*.

Within 10 minutes of any situation that I need to know about – such as emergencies, natural disasters, acts of God, changes in client, customer or personnel situations that have an impact on the health and well-being of the organization and/or the bottom line – I had BETTER know about it. When in doubt, err on the side of letting me know.

No one I know in business likes surprises, including me. Staff was forewarned: don't wait for me to find out; tell me first and within 10 minutes.

What do you need to know in 10 minutes and are you prepared to deal with whatever it is?

20

The Good News and the Bad News

> *"Because things are the way they are,*
> *things will not stay the way they are."*
>   Bertolt Brecht

As I have already stated, I don't care much for surprises. Romantic gestures and significant bequeaths from long-lost relatives aside, surprises in business are not a good thing. As a manager and a supervisor, I prefer my surprises with some warning – or at least open and above board.

There is always learning to be found in a tough situation. For me, beyond the obvious, it reinforces my thinking that, when there is good news and bad news I *ALWAYS* want the bad news and I want it first. Good news is good; bad news, particularly to a manager and leader, is critical. Second, share news – again, especially the bad – in time to do something about it. It might not change the ultimate outcome of a situation, but often there are things you can do to alter the conditions or negotiate a better result.

For example: I was in Death Valley, California, on vacation when the telephone rang in my room. It was a senior manager, apologizing for disturbing me, but standing firmly behind the 10-minute rule. She was calling to tell me that our national sales director and manager of our private-market clients had resigned. It was the first week in February and he would be leaving at the end of the month. It is always bad news when a valued employee chooses to move on. The good news was that the employee agreed to help smooth the transition for new contract managers for his accounts and finish up the month with his clients.

Not so fast: the bad news was that, for some time, he had been under-performing while indiscreetly looking for another opportunity outside the company. Now that he was officially leaving, he had three weeks, if he had not done so already, to copy contracts, customer files, pricing models and anything else he pleased. He could also try to convince clients they were better off moving on with him.

My instinct told me to have this individual clean out his desk and leave immediately. We were inviting trouble. My manager disagreed; as the employee's supervisor, she did not want to lose the value of a transition period. I could not help feeling that it was a mistake but I acquiesced. Unfortunately, I was right. This employee did indeed use the time left to acquire all sorts of proprietary information and try to influence clients to make a change.

A third lesson then is to review your contingency and risk management plans. You do have them, right? I mean Plans B, C, D and E. This includes shoring up your resources, if not exactly circling the wagons; having effective decision-making and communication models in place and instilling in your organization a culture of honesty and integrity. Finally, never stop asking questions, seeking solutions and being prepared.

When you get good news and bad news, are you ready with your plans B, C, D and E?

21
Rumor's Had It!

"Before you speak, ask yourself: Is it kind, is it necessary, is it true, does it improve on the silence?"
Shirdi Sai Baba, Indian saint

"Did you hear about..." is a familiar refrain in every organization and it is not always preceded by a furtive "PSST!" It is, after all, human nature to seek the answers to our questions, to collect data, to analyze information, to draw conclusions and to disseminate our findings. Framed in those terms it sounds practically scientific.

Inquiring minds want to know. The problem is that sometimes our good judgment and intentions are clouded with uncertainty, curiosity or downright meanness. Again, it is that human thing. Hence, the rumor.

A rumor, according to the dictionary is defined as, "a piece of unverified information of uncertain origin, usually spread by word of mouth; a story or statement in general circulation without confirmation or certainty as to facts." There may indeed be a kernel of fact buried at the heart of a rumor, but after generations of retelling and embellishing, not a whole lot can be accurately deemed to be the truth.

What breeds rumors most often are organizational changes,

lack of transparency surrounding management decisions or an overall shortage of communication across an organization. Despite the best intentions and open-door policies, I found the rumor mill can still persist in those scandalous office hotbeds: the lunchroom, over the water cooler and at the copy machine.

It was not until several months after I arrived on the scene as a new CEO that I realized how potent gossip and the organizational grapevine were. These are some examples.

- My appointment as CEO was an open secret within the organization before the announcement was made public and the ink on my contract was dry.
- Within weeks of my starting, two employees made it a point to tell me that one of our senior managers was gay and another cheated on his wife.
- Throughout my entire tenure, there was the ongoing litany about "special deals" that had been made with current and former employees as settlements or hush money for past corporate misdeeds.
- Of course there were all those liaisons between staff members partnering and re-partnering over the years. It was frankly amazing to me that any work had been done at all.

Some of the talk was to be expected, the nature of some of our work being what it was: employee assistance programs, crisis interventions, clinical supervision and counseling provided fertile ground for chatter. It was not altogether unusual for a deputy sheriff to appear in our office with a subpoena or other court-related documents. As I was an unknown quantity within an organization where the average tenure for staff was 11 years, speculation about me was to be expected but not tolerated. At best rumors are inappropriate and counter productive. At worst, they can be dangerous and seriously impede morale. It had to stop.

At the next regular staff meeting, I told the group that, as far as we were concerned, rumor had had it at our company. We started with a rather lively discussion around the personal and professional aspects of gossip. We then divided up and worked in both small and large groups, exploring and analyzing a sample of the most outrageous weekly tabloids from supermarket checkout lines. We also viewed a recorded television entertainment "news" show and followed with a discussion of fact, inference and innuendo.

When we came back together as a whole, we played a game of children's telephone, whispering in each others' ears around the room, and then discussed the altered communication, as well as implications and unintended consequences of rumors. I reiterated to the group that at any time they could come and talk to me about something they knew, heard, were upset about or needed clarification on.

Finally, with a bit of showmanship and a *"Voila!"* I unveiled a large wooden box I had purchased for the occasion. It had a mail slot on the top and a lock and key.

"This is the rumor box," I said. "It will be kept conspicuously on a table in the hallway along with index cards and pens. If a rumor comes your way or if you feel like starting one yourself, stop, write it down and toss it in the box. You don't have to sign your name, though you may want to. I will be the only one with the key and I will check the box every day. If there is a rumor to be addressed, I will do so as soon as I can and let everyone here know when I have an answer."

We mounted a sign reading, "Rumor's Had It!" on the wall above the box and waited to see what staff would contribute.

October 27
"Rumor has it that Mallary was dressed to the nines on Wednesday because she had a job interview!"

Ah! So this was the kind of thing on peoples' minds. The next day I sent out a broadcast voice mail to all staff.

"Here is the latest rumor that's had it. First, I want to thank the writer for the complement. For your information, on Wednesday evening I was invited to the 25th anniversary celebration for the Volunteer Bureau of Greater Danbury and was among those honored for volunteer service to the community. It was a wonderful event, showcasing the contributions of many people and a neat opportunity to spend time with colleagues and friends I had not seen in quite awhile. I received a lovely autographed book as a gift, which is in my office if you'd like to take a look at it."

March 10
"Rumor has it that we did not follow procedure for posting the executive administrative assistant position and that because it reports to the CEO, it's okay."

The position had in fact been vetted through human resources and was announced to staff at an all-hands meeting. The job profile was available to everyone. Internal staff members had approached both human resources and me for discussions about the position however neither the human resources director nor I were going to make those meetings and conversations public. That is exactly what I told staff in my response to the rumor. I was aware that in this particular case, one individual's personal motivation drove the spread of misinformation. I responded and we moved on.

Over the course of time about 25 items appeared in the rumor box and almost all were answered quickly and efficiently. The only exceptions were two that were so blatantly malicious and hurtful to an individual employee that I would not give the author the time or attention s/he obviously craved.

The good news was the undertaking was a success overall. Rumors quieted down; people laughed and did not take themselves as seriously as they had before and a lesson was learned. It is certainly not realistic to expect to eliminate rumors from the workplace but there are things that can be done about them.

- Confront rumors head on. When something comes to your attention, bring it to a standstill and go to the source. Ask for facts and verification; if there are none, then end it there.
- Before you add grist to the mill, ask yourself, "Is there any reason for me to pass this on? What is the benefit? What could be the potential harm?"
- Invite co-workers to bring rumors to the attention of a manager or supervisor. This does not give it credence, but brings it out into the light of day. Use the opportunity to get a good grasp on what is being

said, correct misunderstandings and then, if appropriate, pass on accurate information to the proper resource.

- Maintain ongoing feedback and communication loops and processes in general throughout the organization, so that inaccuracies and gossip can be kept to a minimum.
- When you say, "My door is always open," mean it and be as accessible as possible. This is particularly critical during times of organizational change and staff changes and with respect to job security. In these cases there is no such thing as over-communicating.
- Be clear and upfront about what you can and cannot discuss. Specific personnel issues are almost always private and confidential. Employees should know that by protecting and supporting someone else's rights, they are protecting and supporting their own.
- Rumors feed fear and anxiety and add to an employee's stress. The first step to addressing it is letting people know what your policy is and then demonstrating that you mean business.

Providing real information, abundantly and often, can help to shut down the rumor mill and support an environment of trust and accountability.

What rumors run your business?

22
What is at Risk?

"Great deeds are usually wrought at great risks."
Herodotus

Risk is the possibility of suffering harm or loss; "an element or course involving uncertain danger or hazard." Resilience, on the other hand, is "the ability to recover quickly from illness, change or misfortune." Resilience is not the opposite of risk, but a precursor. If you have strength and resilience, you feel safe and confident to take a risk. They actually go hand in hand.

As a CEO I was always trying to unearth the company risk-takers. They were the ones who demonstrated this characteristic in any number of ways. Is this you and those in your organization?

- Taking a chance
- Doing something new
- Venturing out of their comfort zone
- Challenging the status quo
- Going where they have never traveled before
- Understanding the potential for harm and analyzing the potential for failure
- Recognizing the potential for gain
- Learning something
- Proposing an uncertain outcome

- Making a commitment
- Accepting no guarantees
- Flying without a parachute
- Exposing their vulnerability
- Letting go of preconceived ideas
- Facing isolation at times
- Going public

Of course there were the other individuals, those less certain and perhaps less resilient, who had reasons not to take risks. Is this you and those in your organization?

- "We've never done it before."
- "Nobody has ever done it before."
- "It's too radical. "
- "Staff will never try it."
- "We're not ready."
- "Customers are not ready."
- "You're right but …"
- "It's a good thought, but "
- "It's impossible."
- "But …"

How do you know if an idea/risk is a good/calculated one? You don't always know, so you might want to talk about it, share your thoughts about it, explore it, research it, work on it, have fun with it, play with the possibilities, take responsibility for it, try it on and see how it feels. Then decide.

What have you risked lately?

23

Managing 360 Degrees

> *"Management is, above all, a practice where art, science, and craft meet."*
> Henry Mintzberg

Peter Drucker said that part of a subordinate's task is to enable her boss to perform and a boss's task is to enable her subordinates to perform.

Everyone works for somebody else, even if you have to squint to see that dotted-line connection. Everyone also works with somebody else and, let's face it, there are certain givens about workplace relationships that are common and consistent. In my own experiences and those shared by others, I have found the following to be good suggestions.

- Manage up, down and sideways. While not everyone has direct reports or the formal title of manager, everyone can be a leader and make a difference, in both tangible and intangible ways, in their work environments. Everything you do has an impact on others. Much akin to the butterfly flapping its wings in South America and affecting the weather in New York's Central Park, there is always a ripple effect to our actions, no matter how small or silent. We have a responsibility around that fact.
- More practically, though, others you work with can

have a positive or negative effect on your work and career. A colleague can support you in an important initiative or that person can submarine your every idea. A direct report can call the corporate hotline and file a complaint or chat over the lunch table about what a great help you were on that last assignment. A boss's impact on your career is obvious, but a superior in the organization, even one you do not interact with regularly, can nominate you for an important task force or nix your next promotion. You want to do what is best for others, as well as for yourself.

- Take care of your boss and s/he will take care of you; this is a fact of life in the workplace. Keeping the boss happy is written between the lines of your job description, so don't miss it. This may manifest itself in small ways, such as if you are going to the deli for a sandwich ask if he'd like something, too; or in large ways, such as when she is out of the office, be sure to keep her in the loop, particularly on items that are a high priority.

- Very often your success and your boss's success are directly related to each other. Even in difficult situations, respect the chain of command and work within the system. If the system fails, you do have other options like meeting with human resources or seeking out a trusted colleague or mentor that you can confer with confidentially or "off the record." Just be careful; posing the boss as the enemy or bad guy is not a good thing.

- Appreciation and recognition should come from above – your boss – and if you are lucky it does. Also, recognition and appreciation roll downhill.

Hopefully you are getting kudos from your boss and your boss's boss and others within your chain of command. If not, ask yourself about how you are communicating overall and whether changes should be made. Sometimes you need to take the lead in letting supervisors know what you want and need that will help you to be successful. Think about having that conversation with your boss. Be forewarned that appreciation and recognition do not typically come from below. Do not expect your direct reports to appreciate or thank you for your efforts on their behalf.

At one time I had 12 direct reports who were unique in their own individual ways and needed different things from me, depending on the circumstances. Sometimes it was more guidance, sometimes more leeway; sometimes a gentle poke or prod, sometimes complete hands off. I would take my lead from them, though I trusted my gut. My job was to do the best I could to support them – do what I could do to ensure that they succeeded. And I liked it when they succeeded. It was good for them, good for the organization, and, yes, good for me. Often I intervened on their behalf with other colleagues or the board of directors. On three occasions I saved a senior manager's job. Some of this they knew about, some they did not. That really wasn't the point; as a supervisor I always had their backs. With the rare exception, I was not thanked for my efforts. If truth be told, I had no expectation of it but I would have appreciated it.

The irony is I recall one conversation in particular with one director after she had just finished a difficult meeting with one of her direct reports. She came out shaking her head and said, "I don't understand; it was not easy, but I did this for him and he didn't even thank me!" I thought, "Welcome to my world!"

Whether it's about common courtesy or the annual performance reviews, as a member of an organization, we often juggle a variety of roles and responsibilities. While some are explicit in job profiles and performance matrices, others are implicit and should be understood. Next time we think about the impact of others' behavior on us, perhaps we can think about the impact of our behavior on others.

Yes, it's about the work, and it's about results; it is also about relationships. It would serve us well to remember that we are supposed to be on the same team.

How do you manage 360 degrees?

24

It's Lonely at the Top

> *"I try to take one day at a time, but sometimes several days attack me at once."*
> Jennifer Yane

Today's CEO's, business owners and leaders face an extraordinary challenge. To compete within the current business landscape, you must manage complexity, simultaneously wear multiple hats and be the master of numerous business disciplines. At the same time, you have to maintain clarity of vision, think strategically, stay focused and productive and remain excited about your work. No problem: this is what you dreamed of, what catapults you out of bed in the morning and keeps your blood pumping.

Congratulations! You have made it all the way to the C-Suite. So how are you doing at keeping up with your success?

Unfortunately, the more the world around you is in flux, the more you must be certain about what matters in your life: how you spend our time, who you are connected to and where you are going. As a business leader, you need to constantly condition, motivate and refresh your work style and behavior. You need to be prepared for what's next, especially when you don't know what's next.

Sometimes we could all use some help. The question is, who does the CEO go to for help?

I admit I may be part of an extinct species: the superwoman proudly borne out of the feminist movement, working every day to maintain my own personal and professional Equal Rights Amendment and thinking I can (must?) do it all. With maturity and experience, however, come the wisdom to know I don't have to do it all, or at least not by myself, and I am perfectly comfortable asking for help.

Sometimes, however, you need someone to talk to, someone independent and outside of your chain of command. You need someone without his or her own agenda, who will objectively and confidentially listen and not judge, will gently poke and prod, tell you that it's all about you and mean it. That someone is a coach.

Coaching is about helping leaders get unstuck and transfer their learning into results for their organization. It provides a venue for sorting out the myriad issues that arise; helps strengthen an individual's ability to see his or her personal and professional patterns, create both short- and long-term goals and raise the level of physical, emotional and mental self-care. This is critical because this is where you come first!

The most important aspect of the coaching relationship, I believe, is feedback. How often do any of us get an opportunity to truly see how others see us or to get an honest answer to the question, "So how am I doing?"

I am definitely biased. I was fortunate to have had the great opportunity to work with an executive coach for a year and it was well worth it. It was an insightful experience in personal, as well as professional, ways. For example, I am an introvert. If people do not know me, I may seem cool or standoffish. I am actually shy and that's why I don't particularly care for cocktail parties and similar occasions where small talk is work. Plus, as a logical and analytical thinker, I approach situations differently than others. The result is that I may not immediately recognize that someone may be thinking, "I need a hug," when I am thinking, "I need a solution to the problem."

On a more concrete and practical level, a coach can help resolve conflict with direct reports; negotiate office politics; and identify and address your hot-button issues. A reality check with a coach may also help you to realize that an overused strength can become a liability. Coaching can provide a means of finding your own strengths, (which are many) and development areas, (just like the rest of us), in a safe way that you can hear.

Sometimes we can all use some help. Don't you be shy about seeking it out. It is in your own and your organization's best interest.

Is a coach right for you? How might a coach be an effective resource to you?

25

Hats off to HR!

"An ounce of loyalty is worth a pound of cleverness."
Elbert Hubbard

Many execs know this but just in case you forgot, never underestimate the value of human resources and your human resources director. I was fortunate to have one of the best HR professionals I ever met working for and with me. She was smart and savvy, she knew everything we needed to know or she knew how to get the answer.

Through some of our darkest corporate days, she was there not only for the company, but for me. She pulled no punches, did not tell me just what I wanted to hear and was the most trusted employee in the organization. It gave me a great deal of pride and satisfaction to watch her grow and blossom in her ever-expanding role. As our lives within the organization began to change and become more complex, she was always up to the challenge. She was my greatest resource. I hope she knew how much I appreciated her talents and gifts, wisdom and insights, honesty and support.

Thank you, Cheryl.

Who is your Cheryl?

26

Separate the Message from the Messenger

"Everything is data."
Origin untraceable.

Everyone talks about killing the messenger, or not. The notion of blaming the person who brings bad news is not a new one, dating perhaps as far back as Sophocles in 442 B.C. In the moment, this notion may even seem like a good one. The problem is that, as a leader and manager, you need to know the truth, the whole truth and nothing but the truth in order to do your job and make the best possible decisions.

A learned colleague and I recently had this conversation and we both came away with the same conclusion: I am not sure how many bodies it would take, but if killing the messenger were your approach to disagreeable news, it probably would not take very long for the people around you to tell you only what you wanted to hear, rather than put themselves in danger. Eventually, you would not be able to trust anything you read or heard from anyone. How then could you possibly lead effectively?

That is all beside the point. The lesson here is to learn to separate the messenger from the message. This can be a hard lesson, too, particular when personalities and emotion are involved. The following example is from my own experience.

The more I had gotten to know Franklin the less I liked him. He was bright and articulate and connected to a variety of people in high places. He also operated within a loose ethical framework and seemed more concerned about furthering himself than furthering the organization. His long-time connections in the community had given him a depth and breadth of expertise and I was told I could rely on him as a valuable resource. I also knew, however, he had his own agenda and I did not have a lot of trust in his "objective" views. When he began to share some stories about a number of company employees, I cut him off and did not pay attention.

You guessed it: it was a mistake to ignore what he was telling me. Whatever his motives, means and behavior, his insights were correct. Unfortunately there had been too much other noise around us for me to hear and weigh fairly what he was saying to me.

There is, of course, the reverse of that scenario. There are often people we want to believe in and trust because we can see their commitment to what we were doing. They demonstrate a desire to make a difference and have a working style that often complements our own. Here, too, our feelings cloud our judgment because of a common sense of humor or simply a good rapport between us. As a result there are times we put more faith in their knowledge and abilities than we should, particularly when sometimes they have terrible judgment!

How can you avoid these traps and manage to untangle the message from the messenger and be more objective?

- Trust but verify. Attributed to both Ronald Reagan

and Damon Runyon, this simple phrase means check the situation out further, monitor as you go forward and seek other sources to substantiate facts. Of course, you can just trust, but that may be a bit harder to swallow.

- Do some research yourself. Look for supporting evidence, one way or another. Cross-check the data or circumstances with other examples, conditions or precedents.
- Listen to the information cold to get its full import. When we are hot and bothered the temperature colors both the information and our reasoning.
- Break the information down and look at it from different perspectives.
- Trust your gut. Many times our bodies are an accurate barometer of something intangible in the atmosphere that we may be somehow missing.
- Ask tough questions. Then ask more questions.
- Finally, get the best people around you that you possibly can, listen to them and then make your own decision.

How do your own messages get tangled with the messenger?

27

It's Not Personal, It's Business; It's Not Business, It's Personal

> *"Some problems are so complex that you have to be highly intelligent and well-informed just to be undecided about them."*
> Laurence J. Peter

We had a budget meeting scheduled for first thing in the morning. I told Stan about it to keep him in the loop and invited him to join us, in case he wanted to participate, but said several times that he did not have to be there. Early-morning meetings could be a challenge for him. He kept insisting that he would be there promptly at eight o'clock.

The next day the group came together. I said Stan was going to join us and we would wait a few minutes before we got started. We caught up on a couple of things in the time we waited. It was ten after eight; it was a quarter after. The others wanted to get started and so did I, but he said he was coming. This was not a good thing. Finally, at 8:20, I said, "Let's get started." I was embarrassed because I said he was going to be there and kept the others waiting needlessly. Stan took a hit all around because he had insisted on being there and was not. That cost him, and it reinforced an old pattern of his not being reliable. Plus, I was annoyed. At 8:30, he got into the office and joined us.

Following the meeting, when it was just the two of us in my office, I asked him what happened. "Well, it was raining pretty hard so I took my kids to school, rather than have them wait for the bus."

"You know," I said, "I told you several times you did not have to be there and you insisted. We waited for you and you weren't there. Finally we started without you and then you arrived, 30 minutes late. This makes you look bad and this makes me look bad. All you had to do was call and say you'd be late or could not make it and we would have gone ahead without you."

He shrugged and said, "I was just trying to be a good father." After all, he was telling me, his family was the most important thing.

Time out. I knew it was raining and I knew he was a good father, both of which were beside the point. I also knew staff thought he was someone they could not always count on. If he was going to be a successful manager with credibility, as well as capability, this had to change. I was talking about a performance issue and he made it personal. This was a spot-quiz and he got it wrong.

* * * * *

Sarah had been with the organization for just over three months and it was time for her 90-day evaluation. She seemed to be doing well, yet she had not made a great deal of progress with her early assignments. During much of her time in the job, she had been distracted due to a series of personal issues. In fact, she had been out of the office almost as much as she had been in the office. I did everything

I could to support her and gave her whatever time and resources she needed. From a strict performance standpoint, she had not accomplished very much. As a result, I felt that doing an evaluation at this point wouldn't be fair or in anyone's best interest.

When we met, I told her I was going to extend her probation for another three months in order to give her more time to settle in and attack the tasks at hand. She immediately flared up and began to cry.

"It's not my fault! I've had things going on with ….."

I stopped her. "It's not that you have performed badly. You have not had a whole lot of time to show your stuff. This is really in your best interest."

She did not get it. She insisted that she was not at fault and that I was penalizing her. She would not stop crying. She thought I was her friend and she didn't want to disappoint me. Finally, she set her jaw and said through clenched teeth, "Do whatever you want to do." I wondered if this behavior had worked for her in the past.

* * * * *

Two months into the job I had made plans to have dinner out with two senior managers, Nora and Kate. Nora lived in Washington, D.C., and came into town about once or twice a quarter. She and Kate had been friends for years and Nora and I had been friends for almost as long. Our evening was going to be 25 percent work, 75 percent pleasure, and I was looking forward to it. We would meet at 6 p.m. in my office and go from there.

This seemed to cause quite a stir. The next time he was in the office, one of our all-male board members said to me, "I heard you three had dinner together. You'd better be careful. People will think the women are planning to gang up on the men around here."

* * * * *

When Arthur got promoted and his responsibilities and role within the organization shifted and moved up the organizational chart, he and I began to spend more time together, including calls out of the office. We would pair up on customer service visits, participate together in external workgroups, visit our field offices and hold coordinated meetings with staff, clients and funders.

I was pleased with the rapport that had developed between us. I was perhaps one of the few within the organization who appreciated his sardonic sense of humor. Of course, the rumors were rampant that we were having an affair. (How interesting it was that I *knew* about that, although no one had actually *told* me about it.)

It is ironic that he would have been the first one to tell you that he was getting no free ride. He once joked to someone in front of me, "Everyday is a performance review."

* * * * *

The answer to the question, *"Can you work successfully with friends or other individuals you have a personal relationship with?"* is a resounding, "That depends."

I became CEO at my last organization through a series of

events that started with a friend and colleague telling me that the long-time CEO was planning to retire. Actually, what she said was, "After all this time of advertising, interviewing and deliberation, they have not come up with THE candidate and they have not interviewed a single woman! Why don't you get in touch with them?"

So here I was in the executive office because of my friend Carole and I was her supervisor. In addition, she and her husband had graciously taken my daughter in and put a roof over her head for a month while she waited to move into her new apartment in Washington, D.C. Now I had to have a tough conversation with her about a performance issue. What do I do?

Well, I did what I had to do. We started by talking about "the elephant in the room" and effectively pushed it out the window. (It was a big window.) We realized that we could still be friends and work together if we liked each other and trusted each other, never forgot the tricky boundaries that existed and communicated with each other well and often. And that was what we did. We did not always agree and we did get angry from time to time, but we never forgot what was important. We certainly liked and trusted each other, were on the same side and could absolutely disagree on an issue, but that was okay.

I have worked with several friends, almost all successfully. There are rules to doing this well and the one casualty was when we did not abide by the rules.

- Doing business with friends can be fun and profitable, and sometimes it is because of the relationship that you make the sale. However, you must keep up

your end of the bargain; it is still business.
- Identify explicit expectations that you are both comfortable with. It's okay to say, "No, I cannot do that," and that sets the tone for your transactions.
- Understand what is at risk. Did the friendship come from the business relationship or vice versa? Which is the priority and are you in agreement on that? Can you still be friends if the business relationship ends? If the friendship ends, can you still do business together?
- Ongoing communication is critical. If you hit a bump in the road, talk about it. Chances are it will not go away if you ignore it. You will just keep tripping over it.
- It may not sound very friendly, but you may even prefer to put the parameters of your association in writing. That may eliminate misunderstandings down the road and, after all, this is business!

The one exception was a direct report who I originally met and became friends with before we worked together. As it turned out, the hire was not a good fit and she was counting on the friendship to save her job. In the end it did not work; she resigned and I was relieved. The last time we talked she called me at the office at about 7:30 p.m., hoping to leave a voice mail for me. It was her bad luck that I was still there and picked up the phone. She was clearly unprepared for the real me. She chatted awkwardly for a bit and then we said goodbye, promising to keep in touch. Maybe someday we will.

* * * * *

I am constantly impressed by people who will step up to

the plate, volunteer, take a stand and take a risk. This is both personally and professional gratifying. My expectations for myself and others are often quite high, so when someone comes to me and says, "I want to reach even further," it is music to my ears. I always want everyone to succeed. It is about desire and effort, passion and commitment, caring and daring. How cool is that!

As a leader, who are you that they are who they are? What are you doing that they are acting as they are?

28
Saying Goodbye is as Important as Saying Hello

"While you teach, you learn."
Seneca

Individuals leave organizations for a variety of personal and professional reasons. Some are moving on of their own volition; others are asked to leave. A current employee statistic suggests that people in the workforce today will have up to seven different types of careers in their working lifetimes. I think that sounds about right.

When new employees join a company, they are welcomed, oriented, integrated, assimilated and aligned. I believe you should put the same kind of effort into seeing them off to new challenges and adventures, as well.

Exit interviews can be exceptional opportunities for the organization and the CEO to find out information that might otherwise be difficult, if not impossible, for them to obtain. These interviews are structured conversations with departing employees, usually those who are leaving voluntarily. It can be a suitable means to take a hard look at how an organization is viewed. Since the employees are leaving, they will often be more open than they otherwise would be. Yes, they could be taking a few parting shots; still, you should take maximum advantage of these conversations to capture as much data as possible. One of your ongoing foundational objectives should be to enhance the quality of your employees' work life.

In order to be most effective, the interviewer should be someone who can listen with an open mind and also have the authority to make necessary changes, if need be. It is not difficult to see that, where practical, in small organizations the person at the top is the most appropriate person.

How does this actually work? In our organization, an employee would complete an exit interview form and forward it to the director of human resources and me. We would review it and then the employee and I would meet and discuss his or her responses, talk about any suggestions or ideas s/he might have and anything else s/he wanted to share. All the data from these forms and conversations would be collated and then anonymously aggregated. Twice a year the human resources director and I would meet, review the reports and make recommended changes as appropriate and in concert with other management decisions.

In actual practice, I chose to forgo the exit interview in one instance. This was a senior manager who had completed and submitted the forms. Upon review, I discovered that all of the responses and comments consisted of pointing fingers at others, including me, for everything negative that had happened to him during the previous three years. I felt there was nothing more to be gleaned from that discussion. A direct quote from the comments, addressed specifically to me, was: "You have a lot to learn about supervising people. How could I possibly be successful when you were always holding me accountable for my actions?"

There is another interesting dynamic that occurs in organizations when an individual in a position of significant responsibility or authority leaves. I have often seen it myself. On the one hand they would be canonized.

> "Boy, that Doug could do anything!"
> "This would never have happened if Doug were still here!"
> "We are sure going to miss Doug!"
> "I don't know how we will get along without Doug."

On the other hand, they would be demonized.

> "We all know that everything that went wrong during the past two years was Doug's fault!"
> "Doug dropped the ball on this time and time again."
> "It was Doug's responsibility but he had already checked out."
> "We wouldn't have been in this fix if Doug had done what he was supposed to do."

Let's face it: Doug was neither that wonderful, nor that awful. Yet when someone departs, they tend to become endowed with a superhuman aura, for good or for evil. Sometimes, they take on both, depending upon the circumstances they left behind.

This occurs for a reason: in order for us to manage the gamut of emotions that is attached to saying goodbye. If we denigrate an individual, then we will not miss him because he does not deserve to be missed nor does he deserve our feelings for him. If he rises to sainthood, well, he was always too good for us and of course he would go on to bigger and better things. This means that his leaving was preordained and had nothing to do with us. It certainly was not our fault.

Yes, someone leaves and others are *left behind*. That is the other side of saying goodbye. For the sake of those left behind, we need to remember to do it well, *without rancor or regret, with respect and grace*.

After all, what is it that you want people to take with them when they leave your organization? Hopefully, mixed in that box with their plant, mug, son's drawings, team softball trophy and other personal gear will be:

- Bouquets of fond memories
- Buckets of learning and growth
- Broadened insights and experience
- Baskets of funny stories
- Bunches of good wishes
- And a good word or two about you that they will pass on!

What is in the boxes of employees who leave your organization?

29

Evaluation: The Partner of Effective Decision Making

"Are We There Yet?"
Question asked by every child 10 minutes
after the family sets off on a trip.

I have always been a closet evaluator, trained in the trenches of community development and government grants. In the past, toward the end of every project and program timeline, someone was always asking, "What have you accomplished and how do you know?" It therefore is no surprise that I continue to be intrigued by how businesses handle the question of evaluation.

Just say the word "evaluation," and all sorts of negative images flash through peoples' minds.

- *It is a tedious activity that turns out lots of boring data.*
- *It is the very black-and-white way to measure the success or failure of a program or project, using terms like sampling, instruments, reliability and validity.*
- *It is a statement of indifferent conclusions produced through complicated processes that occur only at a certain time in a certain way.*
- *It is almost always done by outsiders.*

In reality, evaluation is about the systemic collection and analysis of information needed to make decisions. It attempts to determine, as thoroughly and objectively as possible, the relevance, quality and impact of activities in light of their objectives. Evaluation helps us make sound judgments, improve effectiveness and/or inform decisions about the future. Meaningful evaluation and project success rely on realistic stakeholder assumptions and expectations about how and why a project or activity will solve a particular problem, generate new possibilities and make the most of valuable assets.

So, how do you know when you're successful? How do you know if your program or project is performing optimally? How do you know if you have achieved what you set out to? And how do you know if in fact you are *there yet?*

The answer lies in asking good, critical, evaluative questions all along the way. These questions should target inputs, or what you invest in a program in terms of both tangible and intangible resources and assets; outputs, or activities, processes, and individuals involved in executing the plan; and outcomes, or results, specifically what's happened, what's gained, what's changed and what's learned.

There are two different types of evaluation: formative and summative. Formative evaluation helps you to improve what you are doing. It focuses on project activities and short-term yields for monitoring progress and making mid-course corrections as needed. This can be helpful in suggesting improvements to individuals or team members, procedures or processes. For example, how accessible was the new training program to staff members at remote locations? How have changes in the training curriculum enhanced participants' skills in serving customers and clients? What changes are needed in the material distribution channels?

Summative evaluation helps you prove whether what you are doing worked the way you planned, focusing on interim or longer-term outcomes and impacts. The purpose here is to determine the value of efforts, based on results. This can be helpful in describing the effectiveness and quality of the project to funders, shareholders, business partners or senior managers. For example, as a result of the new training program and a streamlined customer service checklist, no callers are kept on hold for longer than two minutes. As a result of the new follow-up procedures implemented by the call center team, there is an increase in customer orders and first quarter sales are up.

Both kinds of evaluation generate information that determines the extent to which your program has had the success you expected and how to move forward.

Running parallel to these two concepts, there are also three dimensions of evaluation.

- Process evaluation, which describes and assesses program materials and activities
- Outcome evaluation, which assesses program achievements and effects
- Impact evaluation, which looks beyond the immediate results of policies, services or activities, to identify long-term as well as unintended program effects

Let's look at an example of these in play. You attend a training seminar on developing your supervisory skills. At the end of the day you complete an evaluation form that asks you questions about the organization, schedule and flow of activities in the training – whether the training met your needs and objectives and whether the instructor was knowledgeable about the topic. This is a process evaluation and addresses what happened at the time of the training.

It is now four weeks after the training, and as a result of your attending that session you now are communicating more often and effectively with your direct reports and have begun convening regular staff meetings. You are doing something differently and that is a result and/or effect of the training. This is the outcome evaluation.

Finally, it is 18 months later. As a result of attending the training session and changing your approach to working with employees, you have a better relationship with all your direct reports, department turnover is down and your staff is more productive. This is the impact evaluation or long-term results.

As some may remember it was in the early 1990's that David Osborne and Ted Gaebler helped launch the era of accountability in government. In their influential book *Reinventing Government* they stated:

- What gets measured gets done.
- If you don't measure results, you can't tell success from failure.
- If you can't see success, you can't reward it.
- If you can't reward success, you're probably rewarding failure.
- If you can't see success, you can't learn from it.

- If you can't recognize failure, you can't correct it.
- If you can demonstrate results, you can win support.

These statements remain *apropos* today. While many myths and (dis)illusions about evaluation persist, there is significant value in assessment, monitoring, responsibility, accountability and recognition. Evaluation is a critical process in any endeavor and leads to learning, feedback, growth and refinement. This is particularly true now when everywhere we turn we are faced with multiple bottom lines and demands for returns on investment.

Evaluation needs to become part of the everyday organizational vernacular. It is about results, but it is also about a deeper level of understanding of what is going on. You might say that when a client renews a contract, that is evaluation enough but you want to know why they chose you. Are you just another benefit to add to the recruitment brochure available to potential employees or are you really making a difference? Can you increase your customer utilization numbers and what are the implications of that for your clients, as well as yourselves? Is what you are doing meaningful and providing value to your clients?

As you develop your evaluation questions and framework, the following elements should be considered.

- The target group(s) in question, such as new supervisors, seasoned managers, parents, students
- The desired outcomes, such as a change in the levels of functioning, behavior, attitude, knowledge or skills
- Reasonable, useful and meaningful outcome indica-

tors for achieving the desired outcome, such as the development of a process for consistent performance evaluations; implementation of peer mediation programs in middle and high schools
- Performance targets, such as 90 percent of annual reviews done on time; reduction in employee turnover rates; fewer incidents of school violence

If all of this seems way too complicated and the semantics are confusing, fall back on what I call the five most important questions in evaluation. These are perhaps the only questions you need to pay attention to.

- **What did we do?** It sounds simplistic, but a clear articulation and consistent understanding of what was accomplished will be helpful to everyone.
- **Have we done what we said we were going to do?** Sometimes you get taken off track. That may or may not be a bad thing, so you need to recognize and acknowledge the fact and comprehend why that happened.
- **How did we do at it?** Were we efficient, effective, at our best, solving the problem, running over budget ...?
- **So what?** What difference does it make? This speaks directly to the impact dimension and long-term results.
- **Now what?** I have often said that if what we are doing is important and makes a difference, there is no finish line. So, what's next? Continue? Revise? Expand? Alter? What?

Finally, don't loose sight of your priorities: relationships, organizational capacity, quality and quantity, innovation, effectiveness, magnitude and satisfaction. After all, what gets measured is *indeed* what matters.

How do you know if you are there yet?

30
How Many Decisions Did You Make Today?

*"She didn't know it couldn't be done,
so she went ahead and did it."*
Mary's Almanac

Decisions are at the heart of organizations and decisions are being made by everyone within organizations. Some of these decisions are routine and inconsequential, while others can have a drastic impact on our lives, our work and the people around us. In this increasingly complex world, the tasks of decision makers are becoming more challenging, perplexing and, yes, nerve-wracking. It is encouraging that more and more employees today understand and consider the ramifications of the decisions they make on the job.

Making the tough choices comes with the territory as CEO. For example, one of the hardest tasks any manager has to do is terminate an employee. Even everyday decisions, however, can be difficult because they involve people and relationships – and of course, to some degree, the bottom line.

When I was faced with a critical organizational decision, I sought input from a variety of resources: staff, colleagues, managers, external peers, board members and significant others. I also paid attention to that feeling in my gut; that can often be a vital piece of data.

People would often accuse me of having made up my mind in advance of asking for their counsel. That was probably the case 25 percent of the time, but for the rest, I truly wanted to review other perspectives, ideas and options. I always knew, though, that the buck stopped here.

Smart decision making integrates understanding the situation, identifying and weighing all the alternatives, appreciating the effect of your actions and being willing to accept both responsibility and accountability for what you do. When faced with your next decision ask yourself the following questions.

- Have I explored all my options?
- What are the advantages and disadvantages of any course of action and do I understand the tradeoffs?
- What are the consequences of my action for myself and others and what will be the impact on key relationships?
- Is my decision consistent with my values?

Finally, recognize that no matter how open and above board you are, you must be prepared to defend your actions, without being defensive.

When making a decision, extra consideration goes a long way. A good decision is never an accident; it is the result of focused attention as well as intention, sincere effort, intelligent direction and skillful execution.

What resources do you have available when it comes to making the tough decisions in your organization?

Culture Is ...

"Use your own best judgment at all times."
The entire Nordstrom's Department Stores policy manual

Norms	Layers	Flexible
Environment	Mix	Increased energy
Rules	Decisions	Giants
Language	Boundaries	Value
Authority delineation	Expressing yourself	Metamorphosis
Roles	"The way we deal with ..."	Well-rounded
Atmosphere	Facilitating	Teamwork
Goals	Explicit	Taking risks
Expectations	Collective	Excellence
The Arts	"On the wall" VS "Off the wall"	Focus
Values		Global
Relationships	Evolving	Friendly
Congruence	Attitude versus behavior	Caring
Yogurt		Interconnected
Kinship	Norms VS Policy	Life force
Relationship standards	Familiarity	Stories
Uniqueness	Power	Covers
Diversity	Influence	Branches
Concept of time	Comfort	Vision
Learning style	Commonality	Accountable
Management style	Attraction	Hold your own weight
"My" zone	Coming Together	Linked, connected
Shorts	Opportunities for input	
Space	Selective	Communication
People	Pulling together	Mentor
Leader	Adapts	Creative
"Like" and "Unlike"	Learn, mean	The impossible isn't
Heading towards a goal	Feedback	Opportunities
	Complex levels	Technology
Understanding	Physical presence	Core

31

Which of these apply to your organization?

32

Culture Comes from the Top

"All leadership is influence."
John C. Maxwell

To be successful in any organization you must understand that organization's culture and norms. Members must acknowledge the norms, practices and policies that surround it to be effective and in particular to effect and support change.

Much has been written about corporate culture, but in my mind it can be simply distilled into the following:

- Culture is a body of learned behaviors in common among the community.
- Culture provides a framework for shaping what we do and how we think.
- People learn culture.

Think about your organization and its own patterns. It's bagels every Tuesday at staff meetings; who eats lunch where and with whom; how promotions are determined; Ruth goes to the CEO to complain if she doesn't like what her boss, Rob, did – and usually gets her way. These are the traditions, customs and codes of behavior that have been developed over the years in an organization. These are the social/organizational norms that collectively support and enable the culture. These norms may be written down or simply known practices and they represent an organization's attitudes, values and beliefs. They are patterns.

When you go below the level that is acceptable in a given organization – as can happen – the community will intervene in some fashion. Behavior will be altered, a new pattern emerges and change will occur. Sometimes two separate issues converge to cause the community or, more likely, the CEO to intervene.

I.
Fridays were casual workdays. The dress of the day was relaxed and informal and perfectly acceptable if you were working in the office and not meeting with clients or customers. In fact, you could contribute a dollar to our fund for a local shelter and wear jeans to the office.

Over the course of several months it became evident to me that casual Friday became anything goes and for a buck you could come to work looking as if you were cleaning out your garage or spending the day at the beach in your cutoffs. It was unacceptable. We were professionals, working for a business and doing meaningful work in the community.

II.
I'm not sure why kitchens can be such bones of contention in small organizations, but ours certainly was. We actually had an ample kitchen with a small dinette table that could seat four cozily, a full-sized refrigerator, a sink, a dishwasher, two microwaves and a toaster oven. People were responsible for cleaning up after themselves when they were in the kitchen, but we also had two staff members

who had taken on the task of cleaning the kitchen on a regular basis in exchange for earning additional personal time.

That people did not wipe crumbs off the counters or grab a sponge to swipe the rings left over from their coffee cups when they put them down was not overly troubling. I chalked up the number of science experiments growing in the recesses of the refrigerator to innovation and creativity. Even the occasional snap, crackle and pop leftover from Cal's reheated slice of pizza last week, once again charring on the bottom of the toaster oven as someone toasted an English muffin, could be called a quirky soundtrack to breakfast at the office. Until the day someone toasted their last cheese sandwich and forgot to turn the oven off and the halls began to fill with thick, grey smoke.

When the smoke finally cleared and we could all breathe again, I called everyone in the training room for an all-hands meeting. Though fuming (in the spirit of the occasion), I remained calm and did not raise my voice. During what was forever to be called the *infamous kitchen meeting*, I let everyone know how I felt and that things were going to change.

First, I tossed the toaster oven in the trash and that was the end of that. Next, I told everyone that, if they could not maintain a reasonably clean and healthy kitchen area, then the kitchen would be closed. Staff had thirty days to get their act together or that would be the end. I shared that in a previous position, a similar incident occurred and a colleague had been severely burned by an office-kitchen fire.

Second, I tackled the dress code – never a popular topic. I

announced that our human resources director would do some research on small-company dress codes and we would have a new, reasonable policy about office attire by the following week. My expectation was that they would follow it. No, I wasn't anyone's mother or the vice principle in charge of discipline. I was, however, managing an organization in need of change and during the hours of 9 a.m. to 5 p.m. I was responsible for everyone's safety and welfare.

* * * * *

For normative change to occur, the social norms of a community have to be assessed, examined and redefined. The goal is an acceptable state of conditions that the members have determined need to exist in order to create a productive and successful environment. Attitudes, beliefs, traditions, customs and behavior will vary according to the make-up of the population, environment and systems in play.

Normative change may also involve examining and redefining policy, those formal written statements that an organization abides by, such as the corporate dress code. Some managers will often say, "Let's create a new policy. Then there wouldn't be this or that problem around here." The challenge is not necessarily to re-write your personnel manual, but to create an environment of awareness, support and action.

I believe that beyond acknowledging the environment around you, culture starts and comes from the top. It is about not only what you say, but also what you do and how you communicate about it. Organizations can recognize the importance of this and come together, sometimes with the help of an independent facilitator, to develop a new set of corporate norms for the future.

In recalling how we, as participating members of the organization, wanted to be, it was not difficult to integrate our thoughts into five statements that would speak to our values, principles, strategies and, hopefully, success. It would serve as that template for action. We printed our "Norms for the Future" on colorful cards, framed them and presented them to each staff member. They were visible throughout the office.

Norms for the Future

- First, we are a business.
- Understand, set and enforce boundaries.
- Share bad news in time to do something about it.
- Listen, speak and act with respect and purpose.
- Hold yourself and others accountable.

By the way, some people never forgave me their flip-flops, halter-tops or cut-offs. The kitchen did get straight and was not closed. Most telling, immediately following the meeting a staff member, who was no fan of mine ("I will not work for anyone except Charles" – my predecessor) poked her head into my office and said, "I admire you for what you did in there. You are direct, say and do what you have to and stand behind your word. It's a nice change." She smiled, probably as surprised as I was, and ducked out.

What is the culture you are creating in your organization?

33

Capacity

"Ability will never catch up with the demand for it."
Confucius

At the start of the fiscal year, our development department conducted a resource assessment of all employees. It consisted of one-on-one interviews with each staff member to gauge how people were spending their time, how tasks and assignments were being allocated, identifying efficiencies or the lack thereof and discovering any gaps that we would need to fill. From this an interesting corporate-wide discussion about skills, capabilities and capacity ensued for quite some time.

The first two issues were actually quite simple to deal with. For some time, we had been talking about creating a summary skills matrix for our staff. Yes, we knew that Fran could type and answer the phones and create whiz-bang PowerPoint presentations. What didn't we know about Fran? We decided to finally find out and surveyed all of our staff members on not only their obvious skills, but their knowledge and expertise in other areas. The results were remarkable and we discovered a well of untapped talent and know how.

Next we looked at our products and services. We currently saw things through the traditional lenses of departments.

But what if we tore down those stove pipes and instead sliced and diced all that we did into an integrated menu of options that allowed for cross fertilization? Again, the results were impressive. By thinking differently we could not only enhance our own competency portfolio, but also become a more comprehensive resource for our customers.

There were obviously choices then to be made. We could not be all things to all people, and why should we try to be? Without loosing sight of our core competencies, we had to make some critical decisions about where and how we would focus our time, attention and resources. This brought us to the question of capacity.

Though there are many definitions of capacity, I think we are most familiar with the idea of "the amount a package, container or system holds or can accommodate." There are only so many days in the week; a bus will hold only so many passengers; and a pound of pasta will only go so far.

But what about John? John is a talented trainer and typically has more than enough work to fill his hours on the job. When a long-term project ends, he has time to take on another assignment. His manager, Joyce, asks him to develop strategic goals to support a new development initiative in his division. His deadline is in two weeks.

Two weeks later, John shows his boss what he has done. Though he has put time in on it, she is disappointed. It shows limited understanding of the challenges ahead and barely scratches the surface of where the team needs to go. He can see her reaction immediately and becomes defensive. He asks her just to tell him what she wants; she tells him she wants *his* thoughts and ideas. This is a familiar scene that has been played out in the past and so they continue to go around and around on this.

This, too, is a capacity issue. Joyce thought two weeks was ample time to complete the task. The truth is two years would not have been long enough. Despite his 21 years on the job and consistently outstanding training evaluations, John did not have the capacity – the ability – to accomplish this job. His combination of strengths and resources was not the right combination for this particular assignment. He was an excellent communicator, facilitator and tactician. He was not someone who thought at 30,000 feet. His strengths were on the ground along with the rest of him. At some level he might have known that. Joyce did not.

When she finally understood where his capacities lay the situation was easily resolved. It taught everyone a lesson about expectations. Capacity is what it is. The answer is to recognize your own capacity and the capacity of others. Then maximize the combination of all strengths and resources available within each individual, organization, community or whole system.

What unknown capacity resides in your organization?

34
Don't Forget to Ask How YOU are Doing

"Sometimes I lie awake at night, and I ask, 'Where have I gone wrong?' Then a voice says to me, 'This is going to take more than one night.'"
Charles Schultz

Engaging with others in positive, constructive relationships and on one's side is critical to survival, as well as growth. Valid, reliable, timely and specific feedback is critical to true learning and achievement. In addition, each of us, particularly those in significant leadership positions, can help establish and support a work environment where people regularly and openly give and receive feedback and use it to improve. My performance as CEO was evaluated by the board of directors based upon specifically identified criteria.

From where I sat, however, that was only one side of the story. I decided to specifically ask my direct reports to evaluate my performance as well. Beginning on the first anniversary of my hire and then every year afterward, I sent all my direct reports a supervisor-evaluation form to complete. Yes, there was a concern that some people would be less than candid, perhaps telling me only what I wanted to hear. Yet after a year, I believed that my direct reports knew enough about me to know that I really wanted candor – and none of them were in danger of loosing their job.

After the evaluations were complete, we would then schedule time as part of our next regular one-on-one meeting to talk about the feedback. There were no wrong answers; it was all data. I truly valued these opportunities for open give and take. They helped me to do a better job and it also strengthened our relationships and our abilities to work together.

I recommend trying this yourself, but offer some thoughts on the process.

- Don't ask the question if you really don't want to know the answer. If you do not approach this in a positive, learning framework, there is the potential for irreparable damage.
- Be prepared to listen and accept the responses you receive. Every once in a while, I would hear whispers of, "If you disagree with Mallary, you'll be sorry." Yet throughout my entire tenure as CEO, when challenged for specific examples of that actually happening, not one instance of retaliation against an employee for disagreeing with the boss was identified. I was prepared to listen to the good and the not-so-good comments.
- Feedback can be situational. Around the time of one anniversary, I had a medium-sized disagreement with one of our directors. He was still smarting from some feedback I had provided him about how he had handled a priority situation and his responses to my evaluation reflected his feelings. When we sat down to talk afterward, he told me if the evaluation had come two weeks earlier or two weeks later, his responses would have been different. He allowed

his emotions to do the talking.
- Now that you know, what are you going to do about it? Start by acknowledging what you have heard. Then decide on what, if any, action you are going to take. If there is something you can fix or will do, then do it. If not, say so and say why not. Offer other solutions or ideas or simply say, "This is the way it is." The worst thing you can do is ask for honest feedback, get it and then ignore it. Your credibility will be gone and so may the potential for a positive, productive relationship with a colleague.

Managing and leading a team should be an open, dynamic process. Professional development and learning does not stop when you land in the C-Suite. The more leaders can prepare to grapple with the challenges of today and tomorrow, the more successful their organizations can be. Creating a context that supports the ongoing development of talent at all levels is a significant contributor to competitive advantage and success.

What are you doing to find out how you are doing?

35
Accountability Counts

> *"What people say, what people do, and what they say they do are entirely different things."*
> Margaret Meade

Critical success factors are our measurement for success, the way we know that we have achieved the results we are seeking. When conducting an assessment of an organization, I want to get a glimpse of everything. Not that everything is a priority or even important, but everything is data and helps create a context within which people work, relate and, hopefully, produce.

One source of valuable information is the performance management and review process. It speaks to a number of key points. What is the job that needs to be done? Can the employee do the job, does s/he have the skills, expertise and resources necessary to be successful? Is the employee motivated to get the job done? When completed, how well was the job accomplished? Beyond that, an effective performance management system identifies a clear connection between the individual's contribution and the success of the organization. Finally, the process should yield the answer to the question: "What's important around here?"

In examining the performance process at small businesses, I am very impressed by individual reviews and progress and the high marks all around. What is perplexing to me is, if everyone is doing so well, why isn't the organization? What is missing is the link, and accountability, between the individual and the organization. Corporate goals need to be aligned with individual goals and objectives and vice versa.

There is no reason to reinvent the wheel. There are a slew of wonderful tools and learning resources available in the business literature, so pick from among the best. I chose Management by Objectives.

Management by objectives (MBOs) was first identified by Peter Drucker in 1954 in his book *The Practice of Management.* This oldie but goodie is a method for identifying, planning and controlling employee efforts with an eye toward individual results rather than activity. A manager and employee come together and agree to a set of objectives for the employee to achieve in a stated period of time to come. These objectives should be *SMART*, a validating method which emerged from the practice of management by objectives. SMART objectives are:

> ***S****pecific*
> ***M****easurable*
> ***A****ttainable*
> ***R****ealistic, and*
> ***T****ime-Related*

Develop your own process for implementing management by objectives. For example, at the beginning of the quarter, a manager and employee meet and identify MBOs for the following three months. Both commit to those objectives, ensuring that they are indeed SMART as well as supportive of corporate goals. Once identified, MBOs are forwarded to human resources, reviewed and placed in the employee's file. At the end of the quarter, the manager and employee meet for a formal status update, and depending upon the situation, MBOs roll over to the next quarter, are modified or dropped. A brief report is then completed and also put in the employee's file.

A sampling of MBOs for a senior manager could include objectives similar to the following.

- Develop an enhanced plan for customer service.
- Revise the corporate procedures and policies for emergencies or crises with clients.
- Review consultant contracts and make changes as appropriate for the new fiscal year.
- Create a customer advisory component for corporate services.
- Ensure that 100 percent of corporate services contracts are signed on time.
- Take the lead and jump start the stalled Midwest project.

In greater detail the last MBO might be expanded as follows:

- Jump start the stalled project by providing leadership to project staff and consultants as evidenced by:
    o Completion of the project website and web services by 4/30;
    o Scheduling of at least two, and completion of at least one, of the four regional seminars;
    o Responding to at least two technical assistance requests via electronic or traditional

        means; and
    o   Revising the project budget.
    o   These components will be completed by June 30.

Some of the items on the list obviously can be completed quickly; others can't. Completion dates can be one month away or one year away. These objectives are derived from corporate strategy, planning, tactical conversations among senior staff members and individual performance goals. By the way, MBOs also provide valuable ongoing documentation for your annual performance review process.

Of course, the question often comes up, what do you do when the people you work with do not meet specific task responsibilities? As a supervisor, you rely on your organization's own performance management system to take over. Then, when necessary, progressive discipline policies and procedures answer for you. Don't forget about the relationships involved. In order to guide yourself, explore options and identify actions that are available to you.

If accountability counts in your organization, there should be an explicit expectation that all staff will be holding each other accountable, too. As an individual in an organization, everyone has a responsibility to make things work. In meeting that responsibility, you need to do the following.

- Pay attention
- Know the standards and expectations
- Act
- Have the necessary conversation, even if it might bring up conflict

Finally, there are expectations for leaders in holding each other and everyone else accountable. In living up to those expectations, try the following as well.

- Be aware of what is going on around you
- Know each other's expectations
- Make corporate needs apparent
- Clarify the differences and priorities of personal, project and corporate needs
- Know your level of authority and then use good judgment
- Trust others' judgments
- Air concerns

How do you make sure that accountability counts in your organization?

36
Glory Days

> *"Well time slips away
> and leaves you with nothing, mister, but
> boring stories of glory days."*
>   Bruce Springsteen

People love to talk about the glory days. At one small company, I have heard nostalgic talk about once upon a time three-piece suits and suspenders being dress of the day; lavish parties and tributes; the start (and end) of a software development subsidiary; and putting in long hours, eating cold pizza in the middle of the night and implementing heroic work-arounds when equipment went down in the wee hours before dawn while trying to put a proposal to bed.

Having been there and done that, I can appreciate the unmistakable, heady sense of camaraderie that ensues with everyone pulling an all-nighter together and cold pizza has had its moments in my life as well. I also know about the wear and tear on our wits, egos and stomach linings, and the toll, real and psychic, that such prolonged insanity takes.

What is wrong with having systems in place so that deadlines are met a day in advance, no one has to stay late and we all eat pizza fresh out of the oven in a cozy Italian restaurant?

What are the ways in which your organization is holding onto the Glory Days that, in fact, were not so glorious?

37

Jockeying for Position

> *"When you have two people you have an organization. When you have three people, you have politics."*
> S.J., Retired CEO, lifetime entrepreneur

One month prior to my officially taking the helm as CEO, I was invited to spend two days at corporate headquarters to sit in on meetings and offer input on the corporate goals for the new fiscal year. While we mingled in the conference room waiting for everyone to settle down and grab a "cuppa," one of the officers, a future direct-report, came up to me and asked if I wanted anything. "I'd love some tea if you can point me in the direction of the kitchen."

He grinned broadly. "Allow me," he said and scurried off to get me my tea, exactly as I liked it. Placing it in front of me, he almost bowed.

This action was not lost on those around us – nudge, nudge, wink, wink – and to this day, I smile when I think of it. It was also the only time he went and got me a cup of tea, but he did make an impression.

Awhile back I read a wonderful article by business guru Marshall Goldsmith about the "suck-up factor." So here it was: I had not even officially started my job, but the behavior had.

When I first assumed the position of CEO and for several weeks following, no one on the senior team wanted to leave the office before I did at the end of the day. They hung around (I'm sure they were working) and waited for me to leave – or at least until someone else went first before they left. Sometimes, when they couldn't stand it any longer, someone burst into my office and blurted out, "I've got open school night tonight and have to leave," or "We have a wake this evening or else I would stay."

I often stayed late, particularly in the early days, when I had a lot to catch up on and no one was waiting at home for me. So it was not a big deal for me to stay if I needed to stay. Finally, after awhile they gave up and left when their day was done. Still, no one wanted to be the first one to leave.

Three months after I started we had our first board of directors meeting. Senior managers were buzzing around waiting for their time on the agenda. Each one had presentations to make to the board. During lunch, my predecessor, now a board member, took me aside. "Well I guess it didn't take long for them to switch their loyalty to you, did it?" he asked, referring to the interactions I had had with my direct reports. "It is interesting to watch them now sucking up to you."

Well, duh! I thought. I'm the boss – and *their* boss. Of course, they would be sucking up to me. When you were the boss they were sucking up to you. Did you think that would not change?

In those days, I was a serious walk-aholic. Every day the alarm went off at 4:25 a.m., and I would get up and out, walking five miles before work. This was my own personal obsession and became common knowledge.

Early in my tenure as CEO, I traveled to San Diego to participate in our annual conference for our Navy clients. I happened to mention that I walk in the mornings, if anyone cared to join me. Sure enough, my direct reports all reported for duty at 6 a.m. to walk with me around Harbor Island. Eventually, we had a nice size group moving smartly as the sun came up, though not always the same faces. I could, however, always count on my regulars. This was one way to put their best foot forward, capturing and keeping my attention.

The truth about the suck-up factor is this: we pretend to despise it but secretly adore it. It's like the puppy that unconditionally welcomes us home at the end of the day and will sit and stay at our feet at our pleasure.

As a supervisor – during those times I tried not to enjoy it too much – I would stop and ask myself, "What is it that I am doing to encourage and enable this kind of behavior? And what, if anything, do I want to do about it?"

What do you know about the suck-up factor in your organization and what do you want to do about it?

38
Seek out Opportunities and People to Laugh With

> *"The wind one morning sprang up from sleep,*
> *Saying, "Now for a frolic, now for a leap!*
> *Now for a madcap galloping chase!*
> *I'll make a commotion in every place!"*
> William Howitt

I always thought of fun as part of my job descriptions. After all, laughter in the workplace is a good thing yielding positive results.

- Boosting morale
- Increasing productivity
- Reducing turnover
- Enhancing corporate culture
- Decreasing stress
- Building teams
- Contributing to a sense of camaraderie
- Burning calories

It doesn't take much thought or effort to find ways to engage your group and deliver a good laugh. However, be sure to recognize that fun is in the eye of the beholder. For example, if I were a sports enthusiast, company outings and activities might include tickets to ball games, sports-themed events or even a company softball team. As a more cerebral individual, I admit I favored a different genre of activities.

- Trivia at staff meetings, such as discovering the origin of S'mores
- Ice-breakers and energizers at meetings, such as asking staff to take 90 seconds and list as many uses for a marshmallow as they can
- This day in history or science or myths and legends about the phases of the moon and how they relate to work
- Seasonal recipes – a personal crowd pleaser
- Company socials
- Contests
- Puzzles
- Project derbies

I did my best to incorporate these into our regular schedule, staff meetings and corporate communications. There was often a prize, such as bubbles, seeds to grow a giant redwood tree, or a set of Hakkapeliittas (the ultimate in winter tires) and there was always food. There were also opportunities to be creative while sharing something of yourself and appreciating others.

One of my favorite corporate celebrations was our traditional Thanksgiving luncheon. Our entire corporate community was invited and usually attended. Business was kept to a minimum and we took time to let our hair down and count our blessings. One year, I asked everyone to bring with them to lunch a haiku they had written to share with the group. The results were remarkable. We collected all of the poems and bound them in a book that was given to everyone. The following are some notable samples.

Protection

Although it is raining ...
I shall never get wet
For I am forever ... eternally ... covered.
K-

Dreamer

Ride on, young dreamer
Ride hard and never look back
And never regret.
G-

December

It's in December
With a friend to remember
"Shop till we Drop" Day!
D-

On Sea

Moon arising on sea
Makes silver threads on ocean
Touch my inner soul.
T-

Just another Thanksgiving at the Tytels

If Thor's dish is full
Of stuffing, then what have I
Put in the turkey?
MT-

What makes you and your organization laugh together?

Our Team

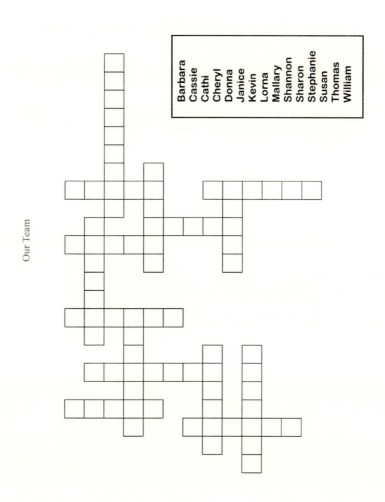

Barbara
Cassie
Cathi
Cheryl
Donna
Janice
Kevin
Lorna
Mallary
Shannon
Sharon
Stephanie
Susan
Thomas
William

Our Team

Barbara
Cassie
Cathi
Cheryl
Donna
Janice
Kevin
Lorna
Mallary
Shannon
Sharon
Stephanie
Susan
Thomas
William

39
Controversy in the Workplace

"To accomplish great things, we must not only act, but also dream; not only plan, but also believe."
Anatole France

Politics, religion, corporate scandals, international conflict. Do your employees feel comfortable talking about controversial subjects in the workplace? While many of us try to avoid controversy and seek quick resolutions, meaningful conflict can be a cornerstone in healthy, successful workplaces and is a must for effective problem solving and open, honest interpersonal relationships.

Controversy is uncomfortable and many individuals do not know how to manage conflict in a positive way. People can get hurt or become defensive and the results may lead to tension in an environment where people must work together and support each other. When effectively managed, controversy and disagreement have many positive results for an organization, including the exploration of different ideas and opinions, better decision-making and a broader scope of options.

According to noted author Peter Block, if you are unwilling or unable to openly and actively articulate the tough subjects, you will never accomplish the things that are important to you at work. Knowing how to raise issues and participate in meaningful conflict is a critical key to success in work and in life.

- Does your organization provide opportunities and support in interpersonal relationships, problem solving, conflict resolution and particularly, non-defensive communication?
- Does your corporate culture promote the notion that differences in ideas and beliefs are welcome and expected, that healthy debate is the expectation and that all opinions are equal?
- Finally, does your organization recognize, reward and thank people who are willing to take a stand and support their position?

If the answer to any of these questions is no, the next question might be:

What can I do to change that?

40

A Matter of Balance

> *"How we spend our days is,*
> *of course, how we spend our lives."*
> Annie Dillard

The role of work has changed. Originally regarded as a matter of necessity and survival, work today is also considered to be a source of personal satisfaction. As individual priorities have shifted, it is no surprise that work-life balance appears to be an important, emergent issue in the workplace today.

Balance is more than a juggling act. It means being in control and feeling comfortable with your choices. While many companies have implemented work-life programs and policies, a significant number have not yet changed their organizational cultures to support employees and managers who want to exercise work-life options. Studies have shown that there is a direct correlation between strong support of work-life balance practices and positive employee retention, productivity and customer service ratings. These are all real bottom-line issues.

When thinking about work-life balance, many people think only within the framework of what the company does for the individual. However, work-life balance has two critical components. The other component, which many people overlook, is what individuals do for themselves in attaining meaning, achievement and enjoyment in everyday life, including work. There are, however, some inherent realities to keep in mind.

- Not everything is of equal importance in your life and perfect balance probably doesn't mean equality.
- Your life is constantly changing and you constantly need to reallocate your resources, such as time, money, energy and attention.
- Things happen that are out of your control but it is up to you to respond to these external forces.
- Change in one area will no doubt impact other areas so be flexible and proactive.
- Recognize and accept that you will probably drop a ball or two now and then.

Take time to explore your corporate and organizational work-life initiatives as part of your overall human resources and employee development practices and policies. Work to actively promote and support the idea that employers and employees share the responsibility. When both company and employee efforts are complimentary and sincere, true work-life balance can be achieved.

What are you doing to contribute to work-life balance in your organization and your own life?

41
You Bring More to Work with You than Your Lunch: One Example

"When we try to pick out anything by itself, we find it hitched to everything else in the Universe."
John Muir

At one time, one-third to one-half of our book of business was providing employee assistance programs to public and private sector clients. Employee assistance programs offer confidential assessment, referral and counseling services to employees and their families who may be experiencing personal or professional problems. Our counselors were often heard saying, "You bring more to work than your lunch and take home more than your briefcase." They were referring to spillover, the premise that a stressor in one part of your life could lead to unpredictable negative effects in another part of your life. The following is one example of the myriad situations you face everyday, the impact that spillover can have on your workplace and some strategies for addressing this particular issue.

A large and fast-growing segment of the workforce – about one out of eight employees – is faced with eldercare responsibility. Eldercare or caring for aging parents affects millions of Americans at an increasingly rapid pace, and this number is expected to triple in the next five to seven years. In addition, in our mobile society, people are more likely to be living far away from the aging parent who now needs their help.

The National Council on Aging, AARP and the insurance industry all agree that caregiving takes a heavy toll on work and family life, particularly for those who provide hands-on care and long-term care assistance. Very often caregivers are stretched to the limit of what they can do; it is no surprise that this spills over into the workplace. The following facts might surprise you.

- Caregiving, when done at home, can add up to 40 hours or more each week of providing care.
- Family caregivers are responsible for coordinating care, including physician visits, transportation, monitoring medications, respite care workers and more.
- The annual cost to employers for lost productivity resulting from eldercare is estimated to be in the tens of billions of dollars.
- Caregiving is emotionally and physically draining and often impacts the quality of an employee's work.
- Eldercare can increase employee absenteeism and turnover.
- Caregivers say that their greatest need is emotional support.

Ignoring the issue is not an option. You can support your employees and colleagues in a number of ways, including some of the following.

- Maintain a culture of compassion, education and

understanding within your organizational ranks.
- Proactively support eldercare issues; provide employees with access to help, information, counseling and professional guidance.
- Develop flexible work schedules and job-sharing programs.
- Be aware and proactive in handling the added stress of eldercare. For example, medical emergencies for the elderly are also generally accompanied by bad news. Be prepared for this added stress for employees.
- Create an environment that supports employees in honoring their elders.

Current demographic trends virtually guarantee that a growing percentage of workers will be faced with eldercare responsibilities in the future. The ripples will affect all of us.

Are you prepared to meet these challenges?

42
Keeping Yourself in the Feedback Loop

"Feedback is the breakfast of champions."
Ken Blanchard and Spencer Johnson

The purpose of professional development is to prepare individuals and potential leaders for the challenges of the business environment. Leadership ability can be learned and creating a context that supports the development of talent can become a source of competitive advantage. Ideally, organizations support learning and not just short-term performance.

A significant piece of the picture that supports leadership potential and enhances true learning is the opportunity for feedback. Having people supporting you, in affirming, productive relationships, is vital to one's survival as well as growth. As previously stated, valid, reliable, timely and specific feedback is critical to true learning and development for everyone. Long-term effectiveness is built on candid feedback and help in learning from errors.

So how does your organization measure up?

You can create a work environment where people regularly and openly receive feedback and use it to improve. First, however, your organization must create conditions that support an effective feedback process. This includes educating your workforce on the true nature of feedback and then offering employees skills training so it can be done well. Here are some tips, for both the feedback giver and receiver, for you to think about in creating a worthwhile process.

- The feedback giver must be a credible source.
- The feedback giver is trustworthy and sincere.
- The feedback is conveyed with good intentions.
- The timing and circumstances of the feedback are appropriate.
- The feedback is given in a personal and interactive manner.
- The feedback message is unambiguous and provides new information.
- The feedback is helpful to the receiver.
- The receiver needs to know how to ask for feedback, whom to ask and when to ask.
- The receiver must be open to feedback.
- The receiver needs to know the right, specific questions to ask.
- The receiver must further learn what to do with the feedback and how to sort out what is useful and what is not.

Understanding how and where talented people can learn and enhance their skills and capabilities is critical and should be accomplished in conjunction with the ongoing natural processes and activities that are already at work within your organization. The primary training ground for the development of leadership skills is on-the-job experience. However, the more proactive an organization is, the healthier the workplace will be. Providing an opportunity within the corporate setting in which others are sought out and encouraged to play an active and productive role in co-worker learning significantly increases the odds of success all around.

What systems do you have in place for the effective sharing of feedback? How well do those systems work?

43

Uncivil Service

> *"I suppose leadership at one time meant muscles; but today it means getting along with people."*
> Mohandas Gandhi

More and more in professional conversations, I am hearing about workplace manners, or the lack thereof. It seems that today's casual business environment has endangered civility, professional courtesy and regard for others, leaving rudeness, disrespect and other inappropriate behaviors in its wake.

Common complaints include interruptions, foul language, gossip, undermining, cliques and caste systems, chronic lateness for meetings and appointments, conflicting directives, missed deadlines, ill-tempered voice mails, flaming e-mails, unreturned phone calls and crossing personal or professional boundaries.

Is your office immune? According to colleagues and fellow consultants, the problem with this kind of behavior is that many people do not recognize that it *is* a problem. However, more and more I am hearing about employees leaving their workplace due to co-workers' and supervisors' bad behavior, and even more are considering quitting because of it. That represents a huge impact on morale, retention and productivity. In the extreme, uncivil workplace behavior can instigate acts of violence and/or costly legal actions.

There are a variety of causes for workplace incivility: overstressed and overworked employees, budget cuts, tension to do more with less, job insecurity, congested environments, fatigue and increasing isolation from one another. Attending to one's attitudes and actions is one way to make a difference and pays off in very big ways. For example, a cooperative study by Harvard University, The Carnegie Foundation and the Stanford Research Institute showed that technical skills account for only 15 percent of why individuals get, keep and advance in the work setting; 85 percent of professional success is related to people skills.

By making civility a priority within your organization and part of your culture, you can help develop more productive and professional work relationships; diffuse hostile work environments; foster mutual feelings of respect between coworkers and supervisors; improve self-esteem and teamwork; enhance problem solving; and increase trust overall in the workplace.

On the macro level, management should model appropriate behavior and accountability. Civility guidelines can be set the same as dress codes or other workplace requirements. You might also consider evaluating and measuring civility like any other performance metric. Working and playing well with others has a significant impact on individual and team performance.

On the micro level, we should all take the time to observe civility in everyday situations.

- Follow the Golden Rule and *do unto others as you*

would have them do unto you.
- Clean up after yourself.
- Don't make promises you cannot keep.
- Be considerate of others' time.
- Return messages.
- Don't hesitate to say "Please," "Thank you," or "I'm sorry."
- Be patient.
- Speak to people as equals.
- Smile.

Finally, seek out opportunities at work to practice random acts of kindness. The time spent showing consideration for others is a smart career and corporate investment. A basic tenet of business etiquette is behaving and communicating in a way in which you would like to be treated yourself. People do tend to have long memories when it comes to how you treat them.

How are you doing unto others?

44

Rituals

> *"I am a part of all that I have met."*
> Alfred Tennyson

Think about your typical day: you take the same route to the office, listen to a specific radio station in the car, buy a newspaper from a particular vendor and exchange a standard joke with the receptionist or security guard. You don your favorite clothes for an important meeting, consistently choose the same mug and reward yourself with a treat for completing a dreaded task.

For the most part you choose to think about work as rational, goal-driven and devoid of sentiment. More and more, however, the research of psychologists, anthropologists and sociologists shows that modern practices and notions of the workplace may be among the most complex ritual systems ever developed. From Monday is Donut Day to Dress Down Friday, familiar practices and rituals support collaboration in the workplace and allow individuals to create meaning in their working lives.

One significant thread in the cultural fabric and tradition of corporations, for example, is the company picnic. For employers, the company picnic is an opportunity to show their appreciation to employees. It may be one of the few times people from different departments and at different levels within the organization can come together in a low-key, fun setting and get to know each other better. The annual picnic is also a great way to demonstrate family-friendly policies.

For employees, the company picnic strengthens the identity of the team, increases camaraderie and renews trust among co-workers. It also provides a venue to communicate and encourage the collective values of importance to the group. According to Dr. Mark Auslander, professor of anthropology at Emory University, "Human beings are a meaning-making and ritual-performing species, and the exclusion of ritual from the workplace tends to have disruptive, even debilitating, consequences."

When rituals are in place and succeed, they allow people and organizations to step out of the ordinary and appreciate, consciously or unconsciously, their shared social bonds and beliefs, as well as each other. More importantly, it is a way for members of a work team to reinforce ties and share ideals and a sense of commitment to what they are doing.

What are the rituals that support and enhance your organization?

45
Managing Time

> *"And when is there time to remember,*
> *to sift, to weigh, to estimate, to total?"*
> Tillie Olsen

I recently completed a coaching assignment with a group of mid-level supervisors. As we talked about goals for the next six to twelve months, almost universally, time management was identified. The common lament: "I start the day with a schedule, to-do list, lots of energy and good intentions. However, all too often, it feels like I am jumping from one crisis to another and at the end of the day, my to-do list is no shorter than it was first thing in the morning. There just aren't enough hours in the day."

Time management refers to the development of processes and tools that increase efficiency and productivity. In the business environment, this can mean everything from enterprise resource planning to professional consultants and organizers. For many people, however, time management is thought of as personal or self-management: wasting less time on doing the things you have to do, so you have more time to do the things you want to do.

According to faculty at the office of organization development and training at Tufts University, effective time management is a conscious decision where we *decide* what is important. This encompasses knowing what you need to do, where you want to end up, what it is you truly value and then planning your time and your life around these things. Time management competencies include goal setting, planning, prioritizing, decision making, delegating and scheduling.

If you've thought about improving your own time management skills, consider the following.

- Keep an activity log. Track your day and find out how you really spend your time. Are there opportunities to eliminate waste? Be sure to note how your energy and stress levels vary throughout the day.
- Prioritize. Ask yourself, what is my objective or goal? In answering reflect on what you enjoy doing, where your strengths lie and how you can be excellent at your job.
- Learn to say "no" and delegate tasks when it is practical and realistic.
- Control your environment; begin to avoid clutter, interruptions and distractions.
- Focus.
- Avoid postponing important or difficult tasks. As the former CEO of one Fortune 100 corporation suggested, "Do the hard things first."
- Schedule appointments with yourself to work on specific tasks or projects and keep those appointments. Also, do what you can to preserve contingency time to handle the unexpected.
- Be sure you understand the difference between urgent and important.

- Think of your effectiveness first, your efficiency second.
- Break a job into small bite-sized pieces; don't procrastinate because it can't all be done at once.
- Throughout the day, periodically stop and ask yourself whether what you're doing is the best use of your time.
- Factor in time for relaxation, renewal, family, friends and fun. Balance is critical; if we do not take care of ourselves we will not have the ability to take care of anything else.
- Remember: it is not possible to please 100 percent of the people 100 percent of the time!

There is no mystery or magic about time management. It takes planning, self-discipline and control until your behavior changes become habit. By managing your time, you provide structure and quality to your life as well as peace of mind.

So, how are you at managing time, or does time manage you?

46
Call a Time Out

"Perhaps now more than ever before, job stress poses a threat to the health of workers and, in turn, to the health of organizations."
The National Institute for Occupational Safety and Health

International conflict, terror alerts, national politics, hurricane season, economic instability – there is plenty to worry about these days. And that's before you finish reading the morning paper. Now add lack of job security, downsizing, reorganizations, heavier workloads, longer hours and increasing overall demands. No wonder you are feeling overwhelmed.

While there are some things you have little or no control over, there are other things that you can do something about. One of those is job stress.

According to the National Institute for Occupational Safety and Health, job stress can be defined as "the harmful physical and emotional responses that occur when the requirements of the job do not match the capabilities, resources or needs of the worker. Job stress can lead to poor health and even injury."

Short-lived or infrequent episodes of stress pose little risk. But when stressful situations go unresolved, the body is kept in a constant state of activation, which increases the rate of wear and tear on biological systems. Ultimately, fatigue or damage results and the ability of the body to repair and defend itself can become seriously compromised. The risk of injury or disease also escalates.

Job stress can be caused by a number of conditions. These include how work tasks are designed, corporate culture, management style, interpersonal relationships, roles and responsibilities on the job, career concerns and environmental conditions. It is no surprise that studies show that stressful working conditions are associated with increased absenteeism, tardiness and employee burnout – all bottom-line issues.

Conversely, studies of stress-conscious workplaces suggest that policies benefiting worker health also benefit the bottom line. These include recognition of employees, opportunities for career development, an organizational culture that values the individual worker and management actions that are consistent with organizational values.

Does your workplace seem stressful? As a manager, try the following.

- Ensure that workload is in line with workers' capabilities and resources.
- Design jobs to provide meaning, stimulation and opportunities for workers to use their skills.
- Clearly define workers' roles and responsibilities.
- Give workers opportunities to participate in decisions and actions affecting their jobs.
- Improve communications; reduce uncertainty about

career development and future employment prospects.
- Provide opportunities for social interaction.
- Establish work schedules that are compatible with demands and responsibilities outside the job.

As an employee, think about what you can do to de-stress everyday.

- Learn to recognize the symptoms of stress.
- Look at your lifestyle and see what can reasonably be changed.
- Exercise, eat right, and get enough rest and sleep.
- Learn relaxation techniques.
- Give up on being perfect; ease up on yourself and others.
- Carve out time just for you.
- Work off anger with activity.
- Prioritize your time and tasks.
- Tackle one thing at a time.
- Give in occasionally.
- Make the first move to be friendly.
- Talk with others when something is bothering you.
- Ask for help when you need it; offer to help others.
- Have fun and LAUGH!

In the war on stress, your organization can win as a healthy workplace.

What steps are you currently taking to achieve that?

47

Making a Difference: A Parable *

> *"We must not, in trying to think about how we can make a big difference, ignore the small daily differences we can make which, over time, add up to big differences that we often cannot foresee."*
> Marian Wright Edelman

One day a man was walking along the seashore. He noticed that during the night many seashells and starfish had washed upon the shore. Thoroughly enjoying the morning sun and cool sea air, the man strolled for miles along the sand.

Far off in the distance, he saw a small figure dancing. The man was joyous that someone was celebrating life in such a grand and uninhibited manner. As he drew closer, however, it became apparent that perhaps the figure was not dancing, but perhaps repeatedly performing some ritual.

Approaching the small figure, the man noticed that it was a child. The girl was methodically picking up starfish from the shore and tossing them back into the surf. The man paused for a moment, puzzled. Then he asked, "Why are you throwing those starfish?"

"If I leave these starfish on the beach," she replied, "the sun will dry them and they will die. So I'm throwing them back into the ocean because I want them to live."

The man was very quiet for a moment, impressed with the child's thoughtfulness. Then he motioned up and down the miles and miles of beach and said, "There must be *millions* of starfish along here! How can you possibly expect to make a difference?"

The young girl pondered the man's words for a moment, then she slowly leaned over, reached down and carefully picked up another starfish from the sand. Pulling back, she arched the starfish gently into the surf.

She turned to the man and smiled. "You may be right," she said, "but I made a difference for that one!"

* * * *

Every day, in large and small ways you make a difference. It might be a smile, a wave, making a decision, writing a letter of recommendation or returning a phone call. Perhaps it is simply by saying "Yes" instead of "No." For each of us, small acts of kindness and caring add up in so many ways. Today, find a moment to push pause, look around you and recognize how you can and do make a difference in the lives of others, at work, at home, at play, in your community and in the world.

And then do one more thing: say thank you, shake someone's hand, give up your seat, tell a personal anecdote, make someone laugh, volunteer, share the crossword puzzle, go out and vote.

It all counts; it all matters.

What are you doing today that might make a difference to someone?

*This story is adapted from *The Star Thrower* by Loren Eiseley.

48

There's No "I" in March Madness

> *"Working together works."*
> Dr. Rob Gilbert

Let's talk about March Madness: that rite of spring when the National Collegiate Athletic Association (NCAA), holds the Men's Division 1 Basketball Championship featuring 65 United States college basketball teams. Worker productivity plunges, there is an increase in sleep loss, and according to the FBI, 52 percent of the $3.5 billion anticipated in NCAA gambling will come from millions of office pools everywhere. But March Madness is also witnessing your favorite teams in action; the exhilaration of dedicated players, relying on each other to get the job done; and each of us feeling like a small part of it – like a part of the team.

A team is a group of individuals collaborating to achieve their common goal and to succeed. The whole is greater than the sum of its parts (members), with each contributing ideas and solutions. Characteristics of effective team members include the following.

- Solid management skills
- The ability to be a team player
- Diplomacy and readiness to negotiate
- Willingness to share the credit of successes

- Effective communication skills
- Listening to others objectively
- Concern for team members
- Recognizing and dealing with conflict constructively
- Valuing the ideas and contributions of others

Yet not every team is effective or successful. We can all think of at least one group or team experience we've been part of where things didn't go exactly as planned. In looking back on those events, we can probably pinpoint some of the obstacles we faced to achieving optimal outcomes.

- Hidden agendas: Is everyone here for the same mutual purpose or are there undercurrents at play?
- Internal conflicts: What are the group dynamics at work and are they taking control over the group? If there is conflict, is it about the task at hand or something else entirely?
- Blurred roles: Do we really understand what we are doing here and how each of us contributes to the success of the whole? What is my contribution, and how can I maximize that?
- Confusion and/or disagreement on the vision, the mission and the goal: Are we in sync in terms of purpose and how that relates to our actions and outcomes? If not, what do we need to do to align ourselves and our roadmap?
- Open communication and honest feedback discouraged: Are there constructive feedback loops in place for the free flow of positive and constructive dialogue and viewpoints? Are we ready to listen to

each other and participate in give and take for the benefit of all?
- Vague or unfair decision-making processes: How are decisions made? Often decision-making responsibility will shift, depending upon the task at hand. Is there an understanding of when and how that happens?
- Ambiguous expectations: Is there clarity and consistency of thought? What do we have to do to get there?
- Meetings or work/practice sessions are dominated by a few individuals: Sometimes it is difficult to leave our titles and credentials at the door. The nature of a team should, however, support the unimpeded exchange of ideas, opinions and expertise. While it is easier said than done, the group should maintain its own operating rules that respect and value everyone.
- Competition vs. cooperation among team members: Aren't we all in this together?
- Lack of accountability: Are we tracking our progress and maintaining integrity of purpose?

Whether as a team member, leader or coach you'll probably be part of another team activity sometime in your future. According to Dr. Norma Noonan, director of the Center for Leadership Studies at Augsburg College, here are some tips for next time.

- Make sure everyone on the team knows exactly what the goals are.
- Team members should have a firm understanding of

their own and others' roles and responsibilities so each person knows who does what.
- Ensure that the team has a variety of work styles among its members, such as the contributor; the collaborator; the communicator; the challenger; and the confidant.
- The team should be empowered to carry out its mission.
- Establish a relaxed work climate, emphasizing collaboration and avoiding stress as much as possible.
- Think about what worked well during your last team experience and apply that learning.
- Think about what did not work well on your last team experience and try to avoid a repeat of that experience as well.
- When it is appropriate, allow decisions to be made by consensus.
- Confront problems in team relationships as soon as they arise; don't let them fester.
- If you have responsibility for oversight, act like a facilitator rather than a boss.
- When the project is done, assess your results and team effectiveness and learn from that experience, too.

Win or loose, being part of a team can be an exciting and gratifying experience for anyone: locations, dates, times, officials, facilities, conflicts, statistics, scores and standings. It makes sense to do it well and perhaps we can all learn something from all our favorite teams.

Besides, as anyone who knows will tell you, "There's nothing better than college basketball."

GO HUSKIES!!

What are you doing to contribute to the team spirit in your organization, game time and all year round?

49

Dialogue for One

"You are the product of your own brainstorm."
Rosemary Konner Steinbaum

The concept of coaching is familiar to all of us. It speaks to the relationship between a professional partner and an individual that creates an environment of learning, honesty, respect and accountability. A coach will pass on knowledge and skills through example, experience, expertise and dialogue. This collaboration motivates both participants to be their best and to achieve extraordinary results inside and outside of the workplace.

While executive coaching is not an option for everyone, there is one person that we all have access to as an adviser, steward and guide, and that is ourselves.

Self-coaching is the ability to seek answers with your own skills and aptitudes and to bridge the gap between where you are and where you want to be through honest self-analysis. It encompasses understanding the values, motivation, goals and commitments that you make to yourself that firmly state that you are taking responsibility for your own success.

Begin with a dialogue for one. Dialogue is more than just talking: it is a deliberate and constructive engagement involving views, values and feelings. This self-talk is already going on inside your head every time you are faced with challenges, conflicts or even simple day-to-day concerns. It produces a running commentary about everything you do and seldom lets anything go by without some comment, remark or evaluation. Now, begin to use this information more deliberately.

For example, think about a recent event or situation that, in all honesty, did not go well. Ask yourself the following questions.

- What happened?
- What did you say to yourself?
- What did you feel at the time and afterwards?
- What did you do in response to the event?
- Are you being honest with yourself in your interpretation?
- Are your responses helping or hurting you?
- What will you do differently next time?

Remember that your self-talk should be truthful and fair to everyone, build good will and better friendships and be beneficial to all. In addition, by paying attention to what you are thinking, you can begin to analyze your own development and progress, while improving your problem solving, decision making and overall learning.

Here are some tips to enhance your own self-coaching practice. I've used a fairly common professional development concern as an example.

- Set goals to work on specific behaviors. *I would like*

- *to be more comfortable speaking in front of large groups of people.*
- Seek out experiences that will help you learn and practice new behaviors. *I will volunteer to present the department's quarterly briefing at the next management team meeting.*
- Identify and address any obstacles to your goals. *Well in advance of the presentation, I will do all my homework, be exceptionally prepared with all the data and complete several trial runs of the material, making sure that all the equipment is running smoothly.*
- Continue to practice new behaviors and elicit support and feedback from others for your efforts. *Now that I've aced my first presentation, I will look for opportunities to participate in other department or corporate events. I will also ask co-workers for comments or suggestions on my style and body language.*
- Review and reassess behavioral changes to help solidify your learning. *I will continue to brainstorm and practice strategies for my continued improvement.*

The virtues of dialogue are courage, empathy, openness, patience, reasonableness and readiness to change. The rewards, too, are many.

When was the last time you had a conversation with yourself? What are you waiting for?

50
Total Quality Leadership

> *"It does not happen all at once.
> There is no instant pudding."*
> W. Edwards Deming

I was recently coaching a group of graduate students when the concepts of total quality management and continuous quality improvement (TQM/CQI), came into our discussion. The philosophy of TQM/CQI is credited to Walter Shewhart, who was a statistician at the Western Electric Hawthorne plant in the 1930's and to his protégé, W. Edwards Deming.

Shewhart developed the concept of statistical process control: continuously identifying and charting variations in manufacturing processes to correct and reduce those variations before defective parts were produced. Over time, Deming expanded upon Shewhart's ideas and developed a framework for management that would make these ideas work in the real world.

These practices focused on consistently conforming to customer requirements and proactively managing quality in every function and activity of an organization. Simply put, there is always room for improvement and management must commit to a mode of operation based on the precepts of total quality and perpetual improvement.

In my coaching practice I am often asked to help someone answer the questions, "How can I be better at what I do?" and "How can I contribute as a leader in my organization?" Starting from an understanding of total quality management and continuous quality improvement, it is not a great stretch to arrive at the notion of total quality leadership (TQL).

The body of business and management literature today contains thousands of volumes on leaders and leadership development. Yet while there is no single universally accepted view, anyone can be a leader and it is clearly a role that leans toward achievement of results and influencing others. Leadership development is also a process that extends over time. I will take a page from Deming's book and offer the following list of recommendations for TQL, with a nuanced emphasis on quality.

- Pursue new, strategic and critical thinking and encourage the same in others.
- Know your business, your purpose and your internal and external customers.
- Set true requirements for both yourself and others around you.
- Actively practice and promote the standard that everyone is responsible and accountable.
- Create and maintain open and effective communication pathways.
- Concentrate on prevention, not correction.
- Know and measure what is important.
- Reduce redundancy, chronic waste and ineffective use of your talents, skills and resources.
- Pursue a continuous strategy for your own personal

and professional learning, growth and improvement.
- Use structure and methodology to your advantage for leveraging your strengths and improving areas of growth.
- Maintain consistency of focus and purpose.
- Use a balanced approach.
- Seek out and obtain continuous feedback.
- Apply learning to all aspects of your life.

Every day we look around us and find examples of things that are done with quality and care as well as examples that fall far short of the mark. Rather than concentrate on what went wrong and who is to blame, let's take a look at ourselves and ask, "How can I commit my talents and skills to improving this particular situation?" and "What can I do to make things better overall for everyone than they are?"

How do you answer these questions for yourself?

51
Gifts of the Season

> *"Anything that has real and lasting value is always a gift from within."*
> Franz Kafka

Not too long ago I was asked to give a presentation on the gift economy to a group of management professionals. How appropriate, I thought, as it was at the end of the year at holiday time. So many people were thinking about gifts: buying, getting, wrapping, mailing, giving, returning, exchanging and re-gifting.

A market or commodity economy is based on exchange or giving in order to receive. What is given returns in a different form to the giver to satisfy a need or want and those who have the most attain status. In a gift economy, participants give away things of value for the shared benefit of the community. Those who give the most to others attain status. The gift economy is about 'agency': everyone has within themselves the capacity to contribute and the community will only grow if everyone passes on the gifts they have received to others.

While the business and social entrepreneurship literature is full of examples of successful gift economies from simple, primitive or small enterprises, one should not be fooled into thinking the system cannot work in more sophisticated or complex environs. Author Lewis Hyde identifies the community of scientists as an example of a system that follows the rules of a gift economy. He said, "The scientists with highest status are not those who possess the most knowledge; they are the ones who have contributed the most to their fields. A scientist of great knowledge, but only minor contributions is almost pitied - his or her career is seen as a waste of talent."

Defining success by what one *gives* rather than what one *has* is certainly not a new practice. It is rooted deep in history and human nature. Therefore, today, at holiday time or anytime, I would like to suggest you add three more items to your gift-giving list.

- Gifts from your head: those things you know something about or have expertise in and would enjoy talking about with others.
- Gifts from your hands: those skills and talents you have to build and create and would like to share with others.
- Gifts from your heart: those things you care deeply about and the one small thing you can to do make a difference in the lives of others.

How are you sharing your gifts inside your organization? How are you celebrating the gifts of others?

52

Matters of the Heart

> *"The head never rules the heart, but just becomes its partner in crime."*
> Mignon McLaughlin

"Smitten!"

No kidding, that was the word he used. Recently, I was having lunch with a colleague, a senior manager being groomed for top management at a midsize Northeast corporation. He shared with me that he had been dating someone at work for awhile and he was indeed smitten with her. In fact, they were quite serious about each other.

Uh, oh! Suddenly there was a flickering, yellow beam in my mind's eye. Was that his career dissipation light? "So how has it been maintaining an office romance?" I asked. "Have there been any problems or issues on the job because of your relationship?"

* * * * *

The truth is the changing world of work, coupled with the increasing expectation of being available 24/7, makes it easy for the lines between employees' personal and professional lives to blur or even disappear. With more and more working singles thrown together everyday in a close environment for long hours, personal bonds are bound to form.

Author and relationship expert Paul Falzone states that one of the best places to meet people is the workplace. "People view dating a co-worker as a safer alternative to other traditional meeting places for singles. In an office setting, you can meet someone and get to know them without the commitment or awkwardness of dating." The data seems to support this. A number of recent workplace surveys indicate that more than 60 percent, and as much as 80 percent, of today's employees have been involved in an office romance.

However, matters of the heart should not be taken lightly and as with any relationship, there are upsides and downsides of office romances. Before taking this particular step with a co-worker, you may want to think about how to avoid some potentially costly bumps in the road ahead.

- Be smart.
    - Does your company have a formal policy on the matter? If so, find out what it is. If not, what behaviors do the corporate culture or social norms support?
    - Be wary of relationships between supervisor and supervisee. Such liaisons could lead to significant problems, not to mention liabilities from claims of favoritism, discrimination or sexual harassment.
    - Think about potential long-term implications. If the relationship is successful what does that mean for your roles, responsibili-

ties and career aspirations, particularly at your present company? If the relationship goes south, could you still work together? How will a break-up affect your jobs, the workplace environment and your relationships with other co-workers?
    - Dating should be for singles only.

- Be respectful.
    - This means to yourself, your partner, your co-workers and the company.
    - Create some simple ground rules for the two of you in the office, being mindful of workplace boundaries.
    - Like it or not, be prepared to honor the same degree of privacy and space you would afford any other colleague.

- Be professional.
    - At work, the priority is WORK. Avoid mooning at each other over the water cooler, sending intimate e-mails back and forth or other inappropriate behavior.
    - Be honest. To tell or not to tell is always the question. If people ask, you can say you are dating, but keep it low-key and limit details. Hearing the information from you can eliminate gossip or rumors. You may also want to let your boss know, so s/he is not caught off guard.
    - Be discrete. Mixing business and pleasure is an individual choice, but your business is

YOUR business and no one else's.

Just so you know, I am not suggesting NOT pursuing a personal relationship with someone at work. After all, I met my husband on the job and we have been together all these many years. What I am saying is you should look before you take that lover's leap.

* * * * *

"So how has it been, maintaining an office romance?" I asked. "Have there been any problems or issues on the job because of your relationship?"

"No," he said. "People know we've been seeing each other but as a couple, we maintain a low profile on the job. We work for two different business units, so our responsibilities and accountabilities do not intersect and we do our best to anticipate potential hazards. If something comes up, we address it and keep management in the loop. Frankly - and I admit selfishly - what with the corporate realignment, shifting priorities and some pretty long work hours, I really appreciate being with someone who not only cares for me, but gets it. Besides," he grinned, "she's wonderful."

I believed him. "Good for you!" I said and wished them all the best.

What are the policies and expectations in your organization concerning "on-the job" romance?

53

Caution: Leadership Ahead

> *"The leadership instinct you are born with is the backbone. You develop the funny bone and the wishbone that go with it."*
> Elaine Agather

What are the things you are doing today to prepare for tomorrow? Well, no doubt the answer is many things that support your organization's financial growth and sustainability, operational excellence, serving internal and external customers well and fostering learning, growth and innovation.

Most of us would agree that incorporated in those critical activities are structured performance management and succession planning – both of which are key drivers of long-term business success. These programs include rating employees, as well as differentiating between "high performance" and "high potential." While high-performance employees do their jobs well, high-potential employees are thought to have the skills and qualities necessary to be the organization's next generation of leaders.

Senior management seems to be waking up to the fact that leadership development is not just a job for the human resources department, but should appropriately fall to the operating managers. Many line managers are now directly responsible for staff planning and development. It is part of their job to recognize subordinates' needs and to provide opportunities for professional development, learning and growth. Managers must do this, even if it means nudging their rising stars into new functional areas or units of the business.

Left on their own, some of these future stars or fast-trackers will realize their full potential. Many up-and-comers, however, need support. This may include gaining specific hard skills, such as operations management or finance, which can be learned in a classroom.

But nurturing leadership presents a different challenge. Developing the more subjective and individual abilities, in different settings and circumstances and with different people, is a more complex matter. This can include everything from dealing with ambiguity to maintaining positive work relationships horizontally and vertically throughout the organization.

Practitioners and co-authors Jeffrey Cohn, Rakesh Khurana and Laura Reeves suggest that a leadership development checklist would help organizations grow their leaders of tomorrow. You may want to include some of the following ideas on your own checklist.

- Create a formal, high-level succession-planning process throughout the company, involving senior executives, human resources and external experts.
- Identify gaps in your organization's talent pool, then seek to fill them; your objective is to expand the depth and breadth of your capacity.

- Involve individual business units in developing their own bench strength.
- Reshuffle rising stars throughout the company, taking care that 'A' players are swapped for other 'A' players.
- Make sure your leadership development program aligns with your overall business strategy, reinforces your company's brand and has support from within the organization.
- Ensure that your board of directors and top management are visible and vocal in their support of these efforts.

Rather than a single, traumatic jolt, succession planning and leadership development can smooth the transition of business responsibilities, authorities and accountabilities within your organization. Thoughtfully executed over time, this process can be carefully orchestrated for optimum success.

How is your organization planning for tomorrow's leadership today?

54

Supervisors, Be All That You Can Be

"The task of leadership is not to put greatness into people, but to elicit it, for the greatness is there already."
John Buchan

It has been said, "Employees join an organization but they leave a supervisor." Lately, when I say this to clients, whether in coaching, leadership training or performance management situations, I see more and more heads nodding in agreement. Supervisors and managers have a tremendous impact on the job satisfaction and productivity of employees. They set the tone and create and maintain the everyday workplace climate. They also have the power to recognize and reward, as well as provide feedback and opportunities for learning and development that most employees are seeking.

Despite the acknowledged importance and value of these responsibilities, many supervisors are still uncertain, untrained or ill-equipped to meet the challenges of their role. When I recently asked colleagues and clients if their current supervisors provided guidance, support and timely feedback to help them work better and more productively, approximately half said, "Yes," while the other half said, "No."

A random sample of these same professionals identified the

following characteristics as essential to being an exceptional supervisor.

- They meet the critical needs of the organization, the employees they direct and the customers they serve.
- They are known for their work ethic and highly ethical behavior; they are therefore trusted by others.
- They practice the Golden Rule, treating people the way most of us want to be treated.
- They maintain a sharp focus on where they are going and what needs to be done.
- They delegate and empower others to be creative, solve their own problems and make decisions.
- They are fair, supportive and concerned for the well-being of others.
- They are committed to life-long learning, growth and development for themselves and those around them.

Think about your own organization: How do your supervisors measure up? What does it mean to be the kind of supervisor we all want to have and/or be? Are almost half of your employees feeling unsupported and dissatisfied and therefore not producing up to par?

Very often, it seems that there is no position within a company that has the greater potential to impact results than that of the supervisor. It is every leader's responsibility within the organization to maintain a strong complement of supervisors in order to achieve success.

What is your organization doing to maintain an outstanding complement of supervisory personnel that will continue to develop, sustain and therefore retain your best and most productive employees?

55

The Contract Compact

> *"The buyer buys the seller not the salt."*
> Anonymous

Many organizations are contract-driven: customers contract with a company to provide specific products or services. Typically, all negotiating and pricing is completed prior to the work. These contracts can be a significant, if not exclusive, source of revenue and an organization's prime assets. Because of their importance, the contract management process should be simple, straightforward and managed well. For example:

- All contracts are assigned to a project specialist who is the dedicated contract manager. The contract manager is a trained professional, who has the required content knowledge as well as the significant experience in providing customer service, technical assistance and management of other professionals.

- The contract manager is the designated point person for each contract and provides consultation, oversight and supervision of the delivery of all contracted services. This includes the fiscal management of the contract, as well as direct supervision of any other staff or consultants providing services to this customer.

- Contracts are assigned to managers based upon a number of factors, including workload, fit with the customer, special skills and geography. Contract assignments may change over time, based on the needs of the customers and the capabilities of the staff.

- As the contract manager may often be out of the office, it is the responsibility of other staff performing this function to be familiar with all contracts in their area. In the absence of the dedicated contract manager, any other manager should be prepared to step in to respond to an immediate request for service or an emergency situation.

- All contracts are reviewed annually using a SWOT analysis: strengths, weaknesses, opportunities and threats. A standard format is used for this to identify the terms of the contract, covered services, fees and profit/loss analysis. A detailed contract report must be completed as part of this review that shows a financial analysis of the contract. Managers must present a detailed justification to continue with any contract that consistently operates at a loss.

- The primary responsibility of the contract manager is to provide customer service to the client. This involves identifying and maintaining key relationships with the customer, proactively responding to problems or service issues and keeping the customer informed of activity on the account. All efforts should be made to get access to the highest-ranking individual possible in the client organization. An annual senior management briefing is one way to accomplish this and should be the goal.

Finally, never loose sight of the *critical underlying elements of contract management.*

Relationships
- Identifying key contacts
- Demonstrating capabilities
- Maintaining ongoing communication

Planning
- Appreciating what matters to the customer
- Defining contract deliverables
- Creating a schedule for service delivery

Outcomes
- Recognizing how the work supports the customer's needs
- Timely and effective execution
- Achieving the desired results

Evaluation
- Using documentation
- Reporting regularly
- Incorporating new data
- Analyzing results and their implications
- Understanding value added, both tangible and intangible

By design, this process should be as user friendly, yet professional, as possible. In point of fact, the regular ongoing contract research and development procedure can be distilled down to four basic questions. Contract managers should ask themselves these questions at least once a month while providing ongoing support to their clients. (After all, they are the experts on their own clients and customers, and businesses need to leverage that intelligence into action.)

Right now – at this moment in time! – when it comes to your client:

- What do you know?
- What ideas do you have?
- What questions do you need to ask?
- What do you then need to do about it?

It should go without saying that the next step is to <u>do it</u>!

Are your managers doing IT?

56
Recognition

"People often say that motivation doesn't last. Well, neither does bathing - that's why we recommend it daily."
Zig Ziglar

We all need to know that we are valued. One "Nice job!" or "Atta girl!" or "Way to go!" can make our day and how easy is that? Recognizing employees and colleagues is not just a nice thing to do. It is an effective way to communicate your appreciation for the efforts and successes of others, while reinforcing those actions and behaviors that make a difference in your organization.

Each of us is motivated in different ways, but all of us respond to positive feedback. For some, the self-satisfaction that comes from doing things well is motivation enough; for others, the driving force may be the recognition of peers and colleagues. In general, recognition is an area where organizations tend to fall short.

Noted authors and business gurus Jim Kouzes and Barry Pozner agree. "Unfortunately, the vast majority of us want more encouragement and appreciation than we get – or give. And often we blame the absence of recognition on a lack of time, the fact that recognition is too 'touchy-feely,' or that we don't feel comfortable giving praise."

The good news is there are simple things we can all do to acknowledge, support and encourage others to perform at their best.

- Set explicit standards. People should know what's important in their organization and what the common values are. Recognition explicitly broadcasts to everyone, "This is what counts around here."
- Expect the best. Standards of the organization should be standards of excellence. Remember that you will often get what you ask for: when you believe in others, even if they don't believe in themselves, your belief in them can yield surprising accomplishments.
- Be specific. Pay attention and when you catch someone doing things right, recognize the significance of those specific achievements and activities, both large and small, for the organization.
- Think personal. Recognition should be special and fit the individual you are acknowledging. Individual contributions can make a world of difference; therefore recognizing the individual should reflect differences, too.
- It's about everyone. Stories of corporate glory and success move us, inspire us and make up the fabric of our organizations. Proud refrains of "Remember when" are familiar to every workplace. When we recognize an employee and share that with all, we motivate not only one person but those around them as well. Recognition is, after all, about not only the individual but also what they have contributed to

the whole.

So, go on, set an example.

What can you do to ensure that those you work with are understood, affirmed, validated and appreciated? What can you do to maintain your own healthy workplace?

57

The 100th Monkey: A Story About Social Change *

> *"We are all islands in a common sea."*
> Anne Morrow Lindberg

The Japanese monkey, Macaca fuscata, had been observed in the wild for a period of over 30 years. In 1952, on the island of Koshima, scientists were providing monkeys with sweet potatoes dropped in the sand. The monkeys liked the taste of the raw sweet potatoes, but they found the dirt unpleasant. An 18-month-old female named Imo found she could solve the problem by washing the potatoes in a nearby stream. She taught this trick to her mother. Her playmates also learned this new way and they taught their mothers, too.

This cultural innovation was gradually picked up by various monkeys before the eyes of the scientists. Between 1952 and 1958, all the young monkeys learned to wash the sandy sweet potatoes to make them more palatable. Only the adults who imitated their children learned this social improvement. Other adults kept eating the dirty sweet potatoes.

Then something startling took place. In the autumn of 1958, a certain number of Koshima monkeys were washing sweet potatoes – the exact number is not known.

Let us suppose that, when the sun rose one morning there were 99 monkeys on Koshima Island who had learned to wash their sweet potatoes. Let's further suppose that, later that morning, the hundredth monkey learned to wash potatoes.

And then it happened ....

By that evening, almost every monkey in the tribe was washing sweet potatoes before eating them. The added energy of this hundredth monkey somehow created an ideological breakthrough!

But notice: A most surprising thing observed by these scientists was that the habit of washing sweet potatoes then jumped over the seas. Colonies of monkeys on other islands and the mainland troop of monkeys at Takasakiyama began washing their sweet potatoes. Thus, when a certain critical number achieves awareness, *this new awareness may be communicated from mind to mind.*

Although the exact number may vary, this **hundredth monkey phenomenon** means that, when only a limited number of people know of a new way, it may remain the conscious property of these people.

But there is a point at which, if only one more person tunes into a new awareness, a field is strengthened, so that this awareness is picked up by almost everyone.

* * * *

In organizations across the country – maybe even yours! – something special is going on. It's not about monkeys and it's not about sweet potatoes. It is about relationships and interrelationships, effort and outcome, intent and impact, commitment and a job well done. All of us every day are taking a leap of faith in creating a critical mass to move ourselves and the world forward.

And then it happens .... respect and fairness, diversity and inclusion, learning and growth, capacity and caring, innovation and change.

What are the skills, understandings and behaviors you want to have shared across your entire organization?

*The book "The Hundredth Monkey," written by Ken Keys, Jr., is not copyrighted. According to the book's preface, "you are asked to reproduce it in whole or in part, to distribute it without charge, in as many languages as possible, to as many people as possible." Some have said this story has been debunked. I hope not, but what do you think?

58

Knowledge Management

"My evil genius Procrastination has whispered me to tarry 'til a more convenient season."
Mary Todd Lincoln

I recently received a call from the CEO of a small, Midwestern corporation. The very sudden and unexpected demise of his long-time executive assistant, Jon, left his entire organization not only in shock, but paralyzed as well. Beyond his own obvious personal loss, he said Jon was the only one who knew where everything was. "We are lost. I don't even know how to access my voice mail," the CEO said.

This is perhaps an extreme example; nonetheless, it speaks to the important issue of knowledge management. Knowledge management can be defined as the process of systematically and actively capturing, organizing, storing and sharing the knowledge and experiences of individuals and groups within an organization. This transformation of data and information into knowledge creates value.

Despite the ongoing priorities of successful recruitment and retention, as well as the importance of preserving corporate memory, many organizations have not specifically addressed the issue of capturing and transferring their corporate knowledge. While we all know that employees leave a workplace for a variety of reasons, we may not recognize that, little by little our ability to continue doing what we are doing walks out the door with them. According to professor Phillip Windley of Brigham Young University, "Too few companies pay much attention to managing their intellectual infrastructure."

Organizations possess two kinds of critical knowledge: explicit knowledge and tacit knowledge. Explicit knowledge is available in policies, procedures, manuals, directories, glossaries and best practice guides. It typically accounts for only 15 to 20 percent of an organization's knowledge assets.

Tacit knowledge resides in people and that typically includes such intangibles as judgment, know-how, values and insights. Tacit knowledge makes up the remaining 80 to 85 percent of an organization's knowledge assets and is much more difficult to collect and organize than what is explicit. Indeed, when it is transferred at all, tacit knowledge is more commonly passed on through coaching, mentoring and job shadowing.

To understand this distinction a bit better, look around you and ask yourself the following.

- To whom do others turn in a crisis?
- Who are the subject-matter experts (SMEs)?
- Who has long-term corporate memory?
- Who is doing a one-of-a-kind job?
- Who has a unique set of skills/knowledge?
- Who carries the ball on major projects?

When you are ready to get serious about knowledge management, consider the following.

- Analyze your organization's demographics to identify your vulnerabilities with the loss of personnel.
- Secure senior management support and resources. If possible identify a champion of the initiative.
- Identify critical knowledge holders and other resources.
- Prepare succession and knowledge transfer plans.
- If possible plan for overlap of incoming and outgoing personnel; this will facilitate mentoring and one-on-one knowledge transfer.
- Extract critical knowledge held by SMEs; make sure there is alignment between process and content of knowledge capture.
- Work with information management and technology experts and corporate librarians to identify methodology, formats, software and retrieval tools.
- Encourage and facilitate strong communities of practice to help disseminate tacit knowledge throughout the organization.
- Establish an expectation of and reward knowledge-sharing.
- Involve departing SMEs in the rewriting of their job descriptions and the selection of successors wherever possible and appropriate.
- Provide extensive hands-on support.
- Over-communicate in order to deal with questions

and anxiety, as well as generate enthusiasm and provide ongoing feedback.

Knowledge management and transfer allow you not only to plan, but also to be prepared for the unforeseen. Be ready.

What knowledge management strategies are you using in your organization? If you are not using any, when and where will you start?

59

Pick of the Litter

"When you first meet your prospective puppy gently roll him over onto his back. Hold him there with one hand on his chest for about 30 seconds. A normal puppy will resist you at first but then accept it. A dominant dog will struggle the entire time. A submissive puppy won't resist and might lick your hand. An independent dog will resist and avoid eye contact. This simple test determines how the puppy accepts stress, handles social situations, and reacts to authority and dominance."
Dog Owners Guide

Not too long ago I was asked by a midsize corporate client to assist in selecting an individual for a significant internal promotion. I met at length with three highly qualified, competent candidates and at the end of the day, I made a recommendation. As it turned out, the client agreed with me and made an offer, but in truth any of the three would have done an excellent job.

Sometimes you are fortunate to have an abundance of talent and skills available to you. Other times, once you are clear about what you are looking for and why, you need to work at identifying the best resource for you.

You know what the characteristics of an ideal prospective hire would be: intelligent, competent, sensitive, curious, spirited, able and confident. These attributes are at the top of your list. What should also be on the list are the basic and specific criteria for success that are non-negotiable and consistent with the organization's mission, values and culture.

- Job understanding: Is there clarification of the role, responsibilities, expectations and accountabilities? This goes beyond a job description and to the heart of how this position is fully integrated and contributes to the organization as a whole.

- Communication skills: As the foundation for successful interpersonal relationships, effective communication is influenced by values, perceptions, assumptions and individual style. Remember that all of these are very personal.

- Planning, coordination and execution: There is a fine, continuous balance between independence and interdependence, considering both macro and micro perspectives, thinking and acting.

- Maintaining priorities and organization: This encompasses time management, self-management, flexibility, versatility, follow-through; decision making and delegating; assessing and managing both urgent and important responsibilities. This is both an art and a science and it is no small feat.

- Fit: Are personal and professional goals and values aligned? Is there consistency between what the organization needs and what the individual offers? What does this individual bring to the team and the overall effort? Is the organizational culture conducive to the individual's success?

- Learning and growth: Does the individual recognize his or her strengths and areas of growth? Will s/he seek opportunities for continuous development and gaining knowledge, as well as expertise?
- Commitment: Is there passion, dedication and meaning for the individual in the work? Is this the right place for this particular individual?

In the end, every hiring decision is made with your own best judgment and with your fingers crossed. There are no guarantees, but if you can see beyond the obvious in your selection process, you can help increase the probability of making a hiring decision that you will not later regret.

Finally, be patient and put your emotions aside. You need the ability to see beyond a warm and fuzzy bundle.

Which of these characteristics do you screen for? How can you improve your hiring practices?

60
So, How Are You?

"I seem to have an awful lot of people inside me."
  Dame Edith Evans

Imagine a long-time, accomplished employee. Everyone who knows him believes he has many strengths and the potential to achieve great things. However, as he has gained more responsibility and authority within the organization, behaviors have emerged that are causing him to derail on his career path. For example, he is at times short with subordinates; appears disengaged and disinterested at team meetings; and acts inappropriately at company functions. These are clearly seen in his overall approach to the changing work environment and his interactions with others.

Each of us strives to form good working relationships. We aspire to be a cooperative and constructive member of the group, to control anger and other counter-productive impulses and to increase our effectiveness with co-workers. We need to be able to separate healthy from unhealthy feelings and turn negative responses into positive ones. This is called ***emotional intelligence.***

Emotional intelligence refers to the constellation of abilities through which people deal with their own emotions and the emotions of others. Based on the work of psychologists

Jack Mayer, Peter Salovey and Daniel Goleman, emotional intelligence focuses on the four basic competencies - self-awareness, social awareness, self-management, and social skills - that influence the way people handle themselves and their relationships with others.

We can probably all recognize someone, who at some point has had a low "emotional intelligence quotient" (EIQ). Those characteristics and/or behaviors may include some of the following.

- Persistent judging, attacking, blaming, interrupting, commanding, criticizing and complaining
- Carrying grudges
- Withholding information
- Making others feel uncomfortable
- Playing games
- Not considering the feelings of others before acting
- Finding it hard or impossible to admit their mistakes or apologize
- Locking themselves into courses of action that go against common sense
- Letting things build up, then blowing up over something relatively minor

For years, managers, educators, human resource professionals and others saw evidence that emotional intelligence, commonly called "people skills," seemed to play an important role in separating average performers from first-rate performers. Supporting this, studies over the last 10 years have found significant evidence of the importance of emotional intelligence in effective leadership and management.

Individuals are always evolving and so one's emotional intelligence quotient can change as well. According to author and educator Steven Hein, anyone can increase his or her emotional intelligence quotient at any point by learning to identify his or her emotions and taking responsibility for those emotions. Some tips to increase emotional intelligence include the following.

- Pay attention to your feelings and track them in a written journal. What patterns do you see?
- Begin expressing your feelings accurately; don't exaggerate them or minimize them.
- Listen to your feelings. For example, when you feel defensive, ask yourself, "What am I defending?"
- Think about the consequences of your actions.
- Balance your feelings and your logic.
- Make changes in areas where there are persistent negative feelings; work to invest more time on activities that have lasting positive feelings.
- Try to understand the feelings of others; listen non-judgmentally.
- Be aware of body language – yours and others.
- Set boundaries with tact and honesty.
- Take some risks.
- Ask for feedback from those around you; others will often see things that you don't.

Emotional intelligence is about having empathy for others. It is about standing up for what you believe in a tactful and respectful way. It is about not jumping to conclusions, but getting the whole picture before you react. The key to emotional intelligence is an understanding of your emotions and the emotions of others and acting in the most appropriate way based on your understanding. Finally, if you don't know how you feel, who does?

What can you do to help yourself and your employees increase their Emotional Intelligence Quotient?

61

Simple Rules

"What is it that matters around here? And if we violate the Simple Rules can we still do our work?"
Royce Holladay

There are certain times or points in our lives – a birthday, work anniversary, New Year's, or start of a new assignment - when we step back from everything around us and reflect. Significant beginnings or other milestones provide us with the natural impetus to look back and look forward. We analyze, examine and review what came before with the notion of learning and gaining insight. We identify, plan, organize, and seek to construct the landscape and outcomes we desire for the future.

A short list of s*imple rules* allows us to get back to basics and create a context for what we value as individuals and organizations.

Simple rules guide behavior and bind an organization together. They are comprised of what we believe and understand about our work, the ways in which we work and the fundamental frameworks that enable us to do our work.

Noted physicist Dr. Stephen Wolfram asserts that the keys to understanding phenomena indeed lie in simple rules and models. "Simple rules can produce fairly complicated behavior," and that has some very important implications for complex systems, such as organizations. Look around: processes based on simple rules occur in every area of human enterprise. Often the rules act primarily as a constraint. But they are also used as a fundamental way of specifying how structures and systems should be created and implemented.

In addition, simple rules serve as performance principles. They are the yardstick by which we measure what we do and how we do it. At my company, Healthy Workplaces, our simple rules are evident and expressed. They are:

- *Be proactive.*
- *Seek out learning and creative opportunities.*
- *Ask questions.*
- *Act with kindness, respect and purpose.*
- *Know what I am/we are about*

Do you know the simple rules in your organization? How do those rules support your own beliefs, values and priorities? Do the rules need to change? Finally, how do the simple rules help you to contribute effectively and lead proactively within your organization?

According to the theory and practice of human systems dynamics you can establish and/or modify your simple rules by thoughtfully addressing the following questions.

- What do we value as an organization?
- What do we want to create in our relationships and organizational structures?
- How do we want to function with each other within

the organization?
- What is important to us?

Simple rules are the foundation of any organization or system, just like yours.

Isn't right now a good a time for you to ask and answer these questions in your organization?

62
Asking the Questions

"Everything you want is just outside your comfort zone."
                    Robert Allen

Look around: the workplace is being transformed by an integrated and global economy. Individuals and organizations worldwide are confronting more turbulent markets, more demanding shareholders and more discerning customers. Everyone is scrambling to meet the challenges of the day.

Strategic planners comprehend that the workforce of the future will be older, be more diverse and incorporate greater numbers of contingent, contract and other non-traditional labor. Beyond the continuous improvement and process reengineering of old, critical success factors today include restructuring and retrenching, mergers and acquisitions, state-of-the-art technology, globalization, transculturalism, multiculturalism, organizational shift, structure redesign, outsourcing, customer management and consolidation. Whew!

What do these changes mean to you in terms of the day-to-day work? Plenty! According to noted author and international human resource consultant Robert Critchley, the old world of work meant having a job, going to an office, climbing the career ladder and maintaining loyalty to the company in exchange for salary, benefits and job security.

Today's world of work is more active than passive, with each of us being responsible for our own careers. The work space is anywhere technology allows. There is a commitment to the work and one's self, rather than the organization. Personal freedom and control are more important than job security. Bosses, managers and employees are being replaced by customers, clients, vendors and *intrapreneurs* – those individuals who operate as an entrepreneur within a larger organization – creating innovative new products and services. Success is directly correlated to the alignment of individual values, goals and competencies.

Where would you place yourself in the current business landscape? Even amidst uncertain economic conditions, now may be just the right time for you to sit down and really think about yourself and your work. How does what you are doing compare to what you would like to be doing? As Critchley suggests in his book, *Rewired, Rehired, or Retired? A Global Guide for the Experienced Worker,* you start with the following simple questions.

- What are the three things you enjoy most in your work?
- Do you have good business and personal relationships?
- Do you make a difference in your job?
- Do you have fun each day?
- Do you have time to do the things you like to do outside of work?
- How would changes in your career impact the significant others in your life?
- What would you like to achieve over the next five

years, and do you have the time, energy and resources to achieve those goals?

The very heart and organization of the work and the composition of the labor force are rapidly changing. "A business world that was once familiar, rational and predictable has become confusing, irrational and illogical," wrote Critchley. As we shift to this new paradigm we must consider "the context of the broad change swirling around us."

Whether we like it or not, or accept it or not, global and organizational transformations are happening every day and the impact of those changes is most readily felt by the workforce.

Do you know where you want to be and how you will get there? Are you prepared for the transition to what's next? Most importantly, how will you know, if you don't start asking the questions?

63

Performance Art

"The real secret of magic lies in the performance."
David Copperfield

Whether I am consulting with clients about executive or high potential coaching, developing leaders, planning or creating and implementing a new training program, I have found that there is often a performance management opportunity somewhere in the equation. When I mention performance management people nod and talk about policies, procedures, compliance and annual reviews. But what exactly is performance management, and how can we do it better?

Performance management includes those activities that lead to the accomplishment of organizational goals in an effective and efficient manner. Performance management can address the functioning of the entire organization, a department or a division. It can also pertain to the procedures and processes that support services, products or operations and employees.

The federal Office of Personnel Management identifies five broad elements in top employee performance management.

- Planning work and setting expectations for performance

- Monitoring performance
- Developing the capacity to perform
- Rating the performance
- Rewarding good performance

Starting from this foundation, you can build a performance-based management framework and it is this framework that will support the strategies and actions of the organization and its members on multiple levels. It will also create a culture of accountability, another term that keeps popping up in conversations with colleagues and customers.

A performance-based management framework would include the following.

- *Incorporating the organization's mission into day-to-day actions.* This means the continuous articulation of and reference to corporate critical success factors, as well as operational goals and objectives.
- *Knowing the expectations of the job.* Job profiles should include standards of performance that are measurable, understandable, verifiable, equitable and achievable.
- *Managing performance in a changing environment.* Building change-management strategies and tactics into standard operating procedures is a smart business practice.
- *Motivation.* Looking beyond recognition and rewards, we need to understand what matters most to employees in order to be successful in the recruitment and retention of the best workers.

- *Providing feedback and communicating well*. This means developing skills, maintaining proficiency with technology and ensuring viable pathways for the exchange of information, resources and energy. In addition, we need to consciously construct and support appropriate feedback loops throughout the organization.
- *Using individual and group strengths*. When using individual and organizational assessments, be sure to pay attention to assets, as well as areas for growth and development.
- *Fostering independent thinking*. By encouraging autonomy, risk taking and innovation, we build organizational capacity and potential.
- *Performance appraisals*. Use and maintain a standard, consistent model that focuses on competencies and results.
- *Corrective action*. No one likes to talk about this, but progressive disciplinary procedures should be in place and carefully followed when they are needed.
- *Praise*. Never underestimate the value of "Good job!" or "Atta boy!"
- *Training*. Learning and growth go hand in hand with corporate results, individual success and preparing for the future.
- *Measuring outcomes*. Creating a balanced scorecard lets you know how you are doing and when and where course corrections may need to occur.

In effective organizations, managers and employees practice good performance management every day. This is achieved through consistency, personal integrity, ethical practices, ownership and asking, "What else can I do?" to meet responsibilities, overcome obstacles, support others and achieve results.

Look around you. Is this your organization? How would you answer the question, "What else can I do?"

64

Business Partners

"Snowflakes are one of nature's most fragile things, but just look at what they can do when they stick together."
Vesta Kelly

Every day your work affords you new and different challenges such as contracts to negotiate, customers to serve, teams to lead, problems to solve and decisions to make. And as you tackle each assignment, from planning to execution, you recognize and appreciate your interdependence with others. It's already been stated that no one individual, group or department has all the necessary talent, skills, resources or time to innovate and succeed in the long run on their own.

So look around you. No matter where you work or what you do, the people around you are your business partners. Some represent formal relationships, some less formal. Some are competitive, some are complementary. But the fact remains that collaboration is often the only realistic way to get the job done.

Collaboration can be defined as a mutually beneficial relationship between two or more parties to achieve common goals. Collaboration typically involves cooperative planning, collective responsibility and shared resources. In addition, there is joint decision making among the key stakeholders in reaching a successful outcome.

Just like your organization, right? Well, I'm not being naïve. I am just offering some food for thought. I believe that stakeholders in any endeavor are interdependent and by virtue of being on the same team they assume joint ownership and collective responsibility for decisions made, work accomplished and results achieved. More simply, it is about relationships and interdependencies within the system; that is to say, you are all in this together.

If this is indeed the case, I suggest the following to help support your business relationships and enhance collaboration in your workplace.

- Include all appropriate groups in the planning and decision-making process.
- Develop a sense of ownership and buy in among all participants.
- Identify measurable long-term and short-term goals.
- Within your own sphere of influence, do what you can to ensure the availability of tools, technology and resources necessary to facilitate success all along the way.
- While acknowledging and supporting existing leadership and management, be open to a variety of possibilities that include shared, rotated, formal and informal levels of responsibility and authority.
- Value, respect and include a diversity of people around the table; this means perspectives, experiences, group norms and attitudes, as well as skills and talents. Recognize also that differences create

movement and progress in thought and deed.
- Be open to involving new groups and individuals as the work moves forward in new directions.
- Capture and measure milestones of progress along the way; provide feedback and course corrections as needed.
- Don't forget about group dynamics, such as developing ongoing mechanisms for maintaining positive working relationships, team building and conflict resolution.
- Deal with obstacles as you bump into them.
- Clearly identify and define everyone's roles and responsibilities.
- Develop a sense of trust and credibility within the group.
- Recognize and celebrate successes together.
- Take pride in your own contributions and the contributions of others.
- Have fun.

Someone recently said to me, "Collaborating is theoretically easy, practically hard and essential for success." I nodded in agreement. It's also well worth the effort.

What are the ways you are building or can build collaboration in your organization?

65

Rules of Engagement

> *"The greatest danger for most of us is not that our aim is too high and we miss it, but that it is too low and we reach it."*
> Michelangelo

I have been doing quite a bit of reading lately on what I'd call the high price of disengagement. No, it's not about the geopolitical pros and cons of global military expansion. Instead, the focus has been on the findings from recently reported studies regarding employee motivation, productivity and engagement.

One study, conducted by Towers Perrin and involving 35,000 workers, echoed a Gallup report published almost two years before. Only about one-fifth of workers today are highly engaged in their jobs; another fifth are actively disengaged; and the rest are not engaged and admit that they "are not as productive as they could be." Set against the present business landscape – international unrest, an uncertain economy, lack of job security, ethical and financial shenanigans in executive suites – this is surely no surprise.

What may be a surprise is the degree to which this affects the bottom line. According to the Society for Human Resource Management, it has been estimated that disengaged workers – those who are basically disconnected from their jobs – cost U.S. employers, like you and me, billions of dollars a year.

An interesting parallel emerged when I conducted a poll earlier this year among a sample of public sector employees. Those interviewed stated quite candidly that they are "on hold," and basically treading water while waiting to see what will happen economically and politically over the next 12 to 15 months.

What are some signs of disengagement? Imagine a star performer who, in the past, did whatever it took to get the job done and who now sits on the sidelines and contributes at a minimal level or not at all. A colleague, who works as an organizational consultant and executive recruiter summed it up. "Disengaged workers are rusted out, rather than burnt out," he said. "The employee has essentially taken their heart out of their work."

What can you do? First, start an open-ended, ongoing conversation with employees and co-workers, asking the following kinds of questions.

- Do you know what is expected of you at work?
- Do you have the resources to do your work to the best of your abilities?
- Do your opinions at work seem to count?
- Does your supervisor, or someone at work, seem to care about you as a person and encourage your development?
- Does the mission or purpose of the company make you feel your job is important?

- Are there opportunities for recognition and rewards for a job well done?
- What is the (implicit or explicit) message you are receiving from your organization's leadership?

Second, pay attention to the answers that you get. They will help you determine employee attitudes and give you a good starting point in determining what needs to be done to re-connect and re-energize your team. (Don't forget to ask yourself these same questions!)

Third, follow through. This is critical. Your actions will speak volumes, telling your employees that you are concerned, are there to help, want them to succeed and mean it!

Motivation is the inner force that drives employee behavior and motivation plus attitude are directly correlated with participation. It is what causes employees to deliver and deliver well on what they say.

What are the ways in which you are increasing engagement among your own employees?

66

Time Off

> *"My advice to you is not to inquire why or whither, but just enjoy your ice cream while it's on your plate -- that's my philosophy."*
> Thornton Wilder

Summer, winter, spring or fall: no matter what time of year, most people agree that taking time off from work is important for both employees and employers. Getting away from daily routines boosts productivity, helps workers gain a fresh perspective and enables them to return to work rejuvenated and prepared to take on new challenges.

And let's face it: you have been looking forward to getting away for months and you have earned it. Ready, set, vacation!

Yes, there is that voice in your head whispering, "Can I go? Should I go? What will happen when I am gone? What will I find when I get back?"

Of course you know that vacations improve the quality of your life and the quality of your work. You return to your desk renewed, refreshed and recharged. The chance to get away from a hectic, demanding job, spend time with family and friends and enjoy leisure activities all contribute to the health-enhancing benefits of time off.

So how do you pull this off successfully? The trick is in the preparation. According to the Work in America Institute, a few simple tips can go a long way to serving all in the workplace.

As a supervisor or manager you can take steps to support your staff.

- Encourage employees to take work-free vacations. Talk up the importance of downtime during one-on-one conversations, in staff meetings and in organization-wide messages.
- Stress that e-mail accessibility is not necessary; leaving a phone number will do. Co-workers and managers will be less likely to disturb a vacationing employee by phone than through the relative ease of sending e-mail.
- Advise staff on planning for accumulating workloads and delegation. Create a user-friendly, reciprocal coverage system among staff members. Keep in mind potential professional development opportunities for individuals who want to try on different roles and responsibilities.
- Be a role model: take your vacation without contacting the office. This is a fine way to demonstrate to staff that you respect their ability to function on their own.
- Establish an explicit company policy for e-mail and voice mail use during vacations. Let both vacationing workers and those back at the office know what your organization's expectations and protocols are.
- Consider it a red flag if an employee seems unable or

unwilling to disconnect. This could be a sign of problems such as poor time management, undue stress or counterproductive pressure from co-workers.

As an employee, you can take steps to ease the impact of your own vacation time.

- Make sure your vacation is scheduled on your company's calendar as far in advance as possible. Hand off your duties to co-workers as appropriate and let others know how your workload will be managed while you're away.
- Prepare a cheat sheet that will include essential tasks that need to be completed during your absence, who they are assigned to and how to locate any necessary documentation or resources essential to getting the job done.
- Set-up your voice mail and e-mail to let folks know you are away. Include information about the dates you will be gone and the person to contact in your absence.
- Plan for the after-vacation period. If possible take an extra day at home to deal with laundry, re-stock the cupboards, reset your internal clock and even get a head start on your work e-mail.
- Once back in the office, reconnect with the boss and co-workers to find out what has been happening while you were away, particularly in your areas of responsibility. Then take time to create a to-do list, prioritizing your tasks and focusing on the most critical ones first. Be sure to thank those who were there while you were gone.

Today, planning for a vacation is as important as actually taking one. It is also a smart way to ensure that your vacation is successful for everyone you work and play with.

Now, go and enjoy!!!

What explicit steps can you and your management team take to assure that your employees enjoy their vacations, and to assure integrity in the organizational fiber during their absence?

67

Help Thyself

"When you are through changing, you are through."
Bruce Barton

Just when you thought you had mastered change, low and behold, here it comes again. From organizations, products and the customers you serve to the foods you should eat and how we communicate across town or across the globe, every facet of our lives is continually in flux. Let's face it: circumstances change at the speed of sight and sound, and every phone call or e-mail announces something has been added, subtracted, multiplied or divided – in other words *changed.*

Even in the best of situations, change can be difficult. The irony is that very often you are helping others handle transitions in their lives; certainly, helping clients manage change is very much a part of what you do every day.

The question is what are you doing for yourself? If the answer is not satisfactory, then it is time to pay attention and make some changes there, too.

- <u>Take good care of yourself</u>. Build up your resistance by practicing positive health habits, such as adequate rest, good nutrition, exercise and a regular schedule.

- Train for change. Practice being flexible by taking different viewpoints, changing your routines periodically and trying something new each day or week.
- Anticipate change. Learn all you can about potential or upcoming change. Imagine your responses to different options. Decide how you might best adjust. Plan for changes in advance wherever possible.
- Avoid impulsive changes. Evaluate all the pros and cons of changes you are considering. Anticipate problems and try to head them off in advance.
- Build safety zones. At times of major change or clusters of change, create a sanctuary for yourself with familiar routines and soothing environments. Maintain an oasis of stability.
- Use a wide-angle lens. Try to look at the broad view of your current situation. Put it in historical perspective. Fifty years from now, who will care? Learn from the past and your past, "I know I'm a survivor!"
- Be flexible. Bend, adapt and don't fight the inevitable. Allow the processes to unfold as they will - even when they take unexpected turns.
- Explore new change-related meanings and feelings. Think about your own reaction to the change. Self awareness is a powerful ally in times of stress.
- Ask advice from veterans. Consult with others who have survived the changes you are currently experiencing. Learn their management secrets.
- Let yourself grieve. Grief accompanies any change as we let go of a past treasure (or even a past pain in

the neck) and move into the uncertainty of a new direction. Take time to grieve. No matter how insignificant the loss seems, grief will be a part of the experience, and grief is a healing process.
- <u>Pace yourself</u>. Don't hurry through the process of change. You'll just add to your stress! Give yourself time to recover and rest. Take your time making decisions.
- <u>Go with the flow</u>. Control is an illusion at best. Recognize that your power lies not in your ability to stand firm and still, but in your capacity to influence and be part of the movement around you. Your actions will be reflected in the shifting landscape as you help yourself and others manage the stress of change.

What are you doing to take care of yourself in the midst of change and what is that modeling for your employees?

68

Learning in Action

"That is what learning is. You suddenly understand something you've understood all your life, but in a new way."
                    Doris Lessing

In today's fast-paced work environment, information escalates and multiplies moment by moment. At the same time your roles and responsibilities shift with each new assignment. Ongoing, lifelong learning is essential. This includes methods and techniques that draw upon workers' experiences; connecting concepts and practices that encourage reflection; and the transfer of knowledge from one situation to another.

One of the best means of knowledge transfer is *action learning,* the systematic process through which individuals learn by doing. Based on the notion that learning and action are mutually dependent, this method engages individuals in "just-in-time" learning by offering experiences and conditions to develop knowledge and understanding when needed. Action learning not only yields solutions to problems and situations, but helps individuals develop appropriate responses to managing change.

In the workplace, learning can often take place in a team environment, supported by ongoing collaboration and communication among members, as well as across the organization.

Learning in the context of the work environment provides the opportunity for workers to clarify their understanding of a situation and reduce the incidence of error.

As an employee, you can enhance learning and development in a number of ways.

- <u>Be Proactive</u>: Take charge of and direct your own learning. Seek opportunities to exercise your independence and self-reliance; don't just sit and wait for things to happen.
- <u>Be Reflective</u>: Introspection augments learning and helps clarify the dimensions and levels of context. Seek expanded experiences, insights and ways of making connections.
- <u>Be Creative</u>: Think beyond what is directly in front of you. Seek out effective ways to challenge the status quo and explore a variety of new and different points of view.

As a supervisor, your attitude and actions around learning and development have a significant impact on employees' growth. You can enhance learning and development across your organization.

- <u>Manage</u> the learning experience, rather than acting as an information provider.
- <u>Teach</u> inquiry skills, decision-making, personal development and self-evaluation.
- <u>Recognize</u> and support diverse personality types and learning styles.
- <u>Encourage</u> critical thinking skills and using tech-

niques, such as field experience and problem-solving.
- <u>Maintain</u> an atmosphere of openness and trust to promote better performance.
- <u>Create</u> opportunities for individuals to use their new skills and knowledge.

How do you measure what you have learned? No matter what formal systems are in place, all of your learning will be gauged by the thoughtful application of what you have gained. Each new draft of a document, field note, interpretation of data, observation, explanation and analysis of phenomena, new project plan or research design, response to a customer, dialogue and discussion you have with direct reports and superiors, every interaction, communication and exchange you have throughout the day, is an application of new learning.

The melding of these actions, in concert with your ability to better think, discuss, teach, act and understand your work and its meaning, is the true value of everything that we know and learn.

What are you learning? If the answer is "nothing," or "very little" then how can you change that situation? If you answered "a lot" then what are you doing to expand this valuable lesson throughout your organization?

69

So You Want to Be an Entrepreneur ...

"Be careful what you wish for, for you will surely get it."
　　　　　　　　Everyone

Dear Mike:

Thank you for your letter. I hope I can answer some of the questions you have about starting your own business. There are many resources available to help you and I will take a stab at it myself. My quick response is the following, which you may have heard before, and is also available from the Small Business Administration. These may sound too basic for you, but you'll be surprised by how much data will be generated by your honest, thoughtful answers.

1. List your reasons for wanting to go into business. Some of the most common reasons for starting a business include the following.
   - You want to be your own boss.
   - You want financial independence.
   - You want creative freedom.
   - You want to fully use your skills and knowledge.

2. Determine what business is right for you. Ask yourself these questions.
   - What do I like to do with my time?
   - What technical skills have I learned or developed?
   - What do others say I am good at?
   - How much time do I have to run a successful business?
   - Do I have any hobbies or interests that are marketable?

3. Identify the niche your business will fill. Conduct the necessary research to answer these questions.
   - Is my idea practical and will it fill a need?
   - What is my competition?
   - What is my business advantage over existing firms?
   - Can I deliver a better quality service?
   - Can I create a demand for my business?

4. In anticipation of a business plan, which you will need if you are seeking outside funding, complete the following checklist.
   - What business am I interested in starting?
   - Who and where are my customers?
   - What services or products will I sell? Where will I be located?
   - What skills and experience do I bring to the business?

- What will be my legal structure?
- What will I name my business?
- What equipment or supplies will I need?
- What insurance coverage will be needed?
- What financing will I need?
- What are my resources?
- How will I compensate myself?

What you now have is a blueprint for proceeding that will detail how your business will be operated, managed and capitalized.

5. Finally, get personal and ask yourself some difficult questions.
    - Is entrepreneurship for me?
    - Am I a self-starter?
    - How well do I get along with different personalities, including vendors, bankers, customers, lawyers, accountants, and such?
    - How good am I at making decisions?
    - Do I have the physical and emotional stamina to run a business?
    - How well do I plan and organize?
    - Is my drive strong enough to maintain my motivation?
    - Significant others: how will my decision affect others in my life?

If you are still undaunted, the next step is to DO IT!!!!!!

I hope this information is helpful. Good luck to you and let me know how it goes!

Regards,

Mallary

Do you possess the entrepreneurial spirit?

PART III
The Big Picture

"The creation of a thousand forests is in one acorn."
Ralph Waldo Emerson

70

Picking Yourself Up

> *"When you get to the end of your rope,*
> *tie a knot and hang on."*
> Franklin D. Roosevelt

I have during my life and particularly of late, considered how people subject to major catastrophes and terrible hardships survived. I discovered it is because of a spectrum of particular characteristics, which, according to Dr. Frederic Flach in his book *Resilience: Discovering a New Strength at Times of Stress,* allow individuals to cope with important, potentially dangerous points in their lives. They are identified as follows.

- Creativity
- The ability to tolerate pain
- Personal insight
- An independence of spirit
- Self-respect
- A capacity for learning
- The ability to make and keep friends
- The freedom to depend on others and maintain a system of support
- A perspective on life that offers opportunities to find meaning
- A genuine give and take in relationships

- Having people we care for and who care for us

Consider the life cycle. It is marked by defining moments, when change is the order of the day. Some of these defining moments are predictable, such as surviving the teenage years, getting married, becoming a parent and retiring. Other milestones or events are not predictable and may appear when we least expect them, such as an adult child returning home to live with Mom and Dad when Mom and Dad least expect it.

Each period of change is stressful and disruptive. They rarely take place without some measure of pain. In fact, they are often accompanied by a degree of uncertainty and risk.

It is our own personal reserves that lie at the heart of human evolution. History is filled with stories of individuals whose greatness was achieved primarily through the resilience with which they met and overcame adversity. But now we live in radically different times. It is one thing to go through periods of personal angst and recover when the world around us is relatively stable. It is quite another when our very foundations continue to be shaken by external events.

I believe that the mark of an intelligent woman is that the more she learns, the more she becomes aware of how much more there is to know. The advance of science, technology and the human condition increases our understanding of the world. In the future, when the record of these times is complete, historians undoubtedly will differ about whether we might have taken different paths. Yet we continue to act, not knowing what will happen to us along the way.

Open the newspaper on any given day and you will see that the world has changed for many of our families, friends and neighbors, near and far, due to natural and man-made events and disasters. Even from a distance, we are often left feeling bruised, battered and uncertain. If we are lucky, the wounds will heal, scar and harden with time. Like another smile line or gray hair, it becomes part of who we are and is reflected back at us through the eyes of the rest of the world. We pick ourselves up, dust ourselves off and start all over again.

The way I see it, we have very little choice but to take responsibility for weathering these storms - through patience, thought, prayer and a resolve to press on. We take one step at a time, sometimes more sure footed than at other times. The point is to keep moving.

How resilient would you say you are? Your employees are? Your organization is? What are the ways in which you are helping yourself and those around you build resilience?

71

Here's to What's Next

> *"Always in motion is the future."*
> Yoda

Welcome to your complex world. Every day you experience a variety of events – from heavy traffic on your drive to work to blizzards in the Northeast – which you ascribe to causal relationships. It is, after all, part of human nature to seek cause and effect.

This serves as a means to your understanding the past, as well as managing the future. While you might not necessarily need to know every detail and nuance of what the future will bring, it would be nice to have the option of being somewhat prepared to make decisions accordingly.

Unfortunately, ambiguity is the order of the day. Uncertainty seems to be the newest "normal" and at certain times of the year we may feel particularly anxious. For example, following holiday cheer and end-of-year financial closings, we are filled with anticipation about the next 12 months – globally and locally, politically and culturally, economically and socially. As our systems become more complex and more open to outside influences, predictability about what happens within the system is diminished, if not completely, lost.

So what can you do to maintain your resiliency and optimism?

You can lead ...

- Believe in what is possible.
- Approach others with unconditional positive regard.
- Maintain an honest ongoing conversation.
- Pay attention.
- Be strategically in sync.
- Be counted on.

You can act ...

- Look to the long-term horizon.
- Focus on hopes and dreams.
- Think about the best-case scenario.
- Seek, recognize and honor small acts of kindness.
- Transfer lessons learned.
- Provide opportunities to reinforce community and meaning in people's lives.

You can develop yourself ...

- Acquire confidence, the state or quality of being certain.
- Acquire competence, standing qualified, physically and intellectually, with a specific range of skills, knowledge and ability.
- Acquire capacity, maintaining your innate potential for growth, learning, development and accomplishment.

Paul Valery stated, "The trouble with our times is that the future is not what it used to be." That may be the case, but it is yours if you choose to embrace it.

What are the ways you are leading into an uncertain future?

72

Know Yourself

> *"He who knows others is wise, but he who knows himself is enlightened."*
> Lao Tze

At the entrance to the Temple of Apollo at Delphi, one of the most sacred places in the ancient world, is the simple inscription, "Know Thyself." Indeed, throughout the ages, philosophers and spiritual leaders have been saying the very same thing. You may also have heard this sound advice from those in your life who care about you and your well-being.

Knowing oneself is no easy task; for most people, it is a lifelong endeavor. However, it is usually at the beginning of a new year or other formal milestone that you pause and take time for introspection and reflection, looking back on where you've been and looking forward to where you are going. At moments like these, you may begin to form a personal plan: you want things to be different.

Now I am NOT talking about New Year's resolutions. I resist making resolutions, but in case you are interested here are the top 10 resolutions for any given year.

- Read 50 books.
- Exercise regularly.

- Drink more water.
- Start a journal.
- Stop procrastinating.
- Visit 12 new places in my city.
- Stop biting my nails.
- Practice yoga.
- Read the entire Bible.
- Be more social.

What I am talking about is self-assessment and awareness: an understanding of what's important to you, what you want and why. If you are game, you may want to consider exploring the following questions and see where the answers lead you.

- What do I want to spend my days doing?
- What do I like thinking, learning and talking about?
- What kind of environment do I find most supportive, empowering and encouraging?
- What kind of people do I want to work with, for or around?
- What kind of lifestyle would I like?
- How much time do I want for myself, friends and family?
- What can I do best?
- What do I enjoy best?
- What motivates me to do my best?
- What type of organization and community would I like to be part of?
- How can I contribute and create value for others?
- Where do I want to be a year from now?
- Where and how do the personal me and the professional me come together or drift apart?

Your values and beliefs influence your decisions and actions. But the important conversations you have with yourself and others and the critical choices you make are about more than results or means and ends.

At the end of the day, I think it is about who you are and what you want to have accomplished.

Take time to ask yourself these questions and identify steps you can take to increase your own self-knowledge. What are you doing to support your team in increasing their own self-knowledge?

73
Being There

"Shift happens!"
Human Systems Dynamics Practitioner

Have you ever been a "fly on the wall?" This phrase, originally coined in the early 1920's, alludes to the concept of "being able to freely observe a situation without being noticed." The idea is to avoid having an affect on the behavior of others who are present.

Well, I do not believe it; there is no such thing as simply being a fly on the wall in my book. Chaos theory seeks to explain complex and unpredictable behavior in systems, particularly when systems are sensitive to the connections, relationships and conditions among members and other parts of the system. A common example is known as the theory of the butterfly effect, which states that if a butterfly flaps its wings in South America, then the weather in New York City, thousands of miles away, will be affected. Theoretically, then it is possible that even the tiniest action can lead to unpredictable or even radical (though not necessarily negative) results through a series of ensuing and seemingly unrelated events.

Not convinced? Then place yourself in these two scenarios:

I. Your daughter is performing in her school's spring

recital. You are hoping to attend because you want to and because it will mean a great deal to her. You told her you would try your best to be there. A few minutes after the show starts, you slip into the darkened auditorium. No one can see you in particular. The people sitting next to you have not missed a note and your daughter does not alter one rehearsed step. Your just being there in a back row has made a difference, even though – in theory – you have not changed a single thing with regard to the behaviors of the participants present.

II. You are giving a briefing to your colleagues and staff on a new product design roll-out. You are comfortable, well-prepared and mid-way through your presentation when the CEO quietly walks in and takes a seat out of the view of most of the others in the room. She sits for a few minutes, nods once or twice, then exits as silently as she came in. In theory she has not changed the behaviors of the participants in the room. However, her presence, even for that brief time, has made a difference.

In both situations, we can appreciate that several things have shifted within the system despite the absence of turbulence. One of those is the misinterpreted dynamic of power.

Power is the ability to move others to do what we want them to do, when and how we want them to do it. We recognize different types of power: positional, referent, personal, persuasive, reward/penalty or expert. All of these are explicitly about authority, responsibility and control.

The rub is that all of these are finite. I maintain that control is, at best, an illusion, often at the whims of natural disaster, hostile takeovers or other acts of God or man. On the other hand, what is truly powerful in complex systems is the infinite ability to *influence*. Picture the ripples of a pond in your mind: one thing can and often does lead to another and another and another, especially in complex systems.

Of course to influence you have to *be there*, whether it is as a fly on the wall or flying off the wall. Being there is what counts and our real power is our *presence*. It is evident in the myriad ways we speak and listen; the countless ways we act and observe; and the immeasurable ways we give and receive every day, contributing to the greater whole.

With this in mind, our overarching goals might be:

- To build diversity and capacity
- To intensify our exchanges between and among each other
- To explore boundaries
- To appreciate differences that make a difference
- To be present, through introspection, reflection and collaboration

Being there and participating are responsibilities that are simultaneous and continuous for each individual within a system. If you are present, you can influence and therefore make an infinite difference in the status quo.

Consider the impact your presence has in your organization, in your work, in your home and religious/community engagement.

74

The Big Picture

> *"The Big Picture is all there is."*
> Mallary Tytel

My friend Joan and I are taking a hike. We set out at first light and our plan is to make it to the mountains ahead in the mist by evening. As I walk on, I focus straight ahead: the clear blue sky, the jutting line of the mountain peak, how the distance slowly diminishes as we cross the terrain. I never loose sight of where we are going; my vision is fixed. However, I am tripping over roots and fallen branches, rocks that have sunk into our path and clumps of mud and grass. I also seem to step into every puddle and creek; my shoes and socks are soggy and my ankles are scraped. Yet slowly but surely I am getting us to our destination.

Joan, on the other hand, is surefooted and purposeful. Her feet set firmly down on the dry path, confident and precise, clearly navigating her way through the debris and the damp terrain. With her eyes focused downward, she scrutinizes every step she takes and her feet land true. Of course, she does veer off course and has twice bumped into trees. Every so often, I gently tug her sleeve to keep her on target.

Is one hiker's approach better than another? It depends upon your character, style and comfort zone. It depends on where you are going and how you want to get there. It depends on your mission, purpose and values. It depends on whether you are concentrating on the Big Picture from 25,000 feet or down in the weeds, seeing every detail precisely in place on the ground before you.

The truth is, both approaches are necessary for success. You cannot be completely one way or the other; that is neither realistic nor practical. An organization will not function with only one type of thinking, personality style or expertise. Diversity and balance are required.

The tension lies in weighing the following questions for yourself and your own organization.

- How do we get to the big picture while focusing on the here and now?
- How do we accomplish the here and now while focusing on the big picture?

Your answers are found in how your company, as any complex system, organizes itself. Look around and you will see what I mean. On one end of the spectrum, personnel and accounting are extremely structured and detail oriented with policies and procedures, compliance and regulations. And you want it that way. On the other extreme are your research and development departments, crisis hot lines, emergency services groups and strategic planning teams: learned, well-prepared, extremely fluid and innovative. There are few rules and more risk taking as individuals creatively pursue their vision and mission, doing whatever needs to be done.

Written between the lines of the CEO's job description is

not only the responsibility to mediate and mitigate this tension, but to achieve movement within the organization as the vision, mission and strategy dictates. It is in this middle space where you seek balance between control and chaos, agreement and certainty. Your goal is self-organization, which allows for the ebb and flow of learning, growth and change to emerge and flourish.

Implicit, if not explicit, is the need to steadfastly hold your line of sight on the big picture: to step back and view the entire landscape with wisdom and passion. The reward is waiting for you. The beauty and mystery of the big picture is that it can be seen with the mind, rather than through the eyes alone.

Which kind of hiker are you? How can you be sure that both styles are present in your leadership?

75

Vision Driven

> *"Success is not the result of spontaneous combustion. You must first set yourself on fire."*
> Fred Shero

In 2001, my husband had open heart surgery. At seven o'clock in the morning, I kissed him and said, "See you later," and he was taken to the operating room. Nine hours and five by-passes later, he was in the recovery room, awake, half-sitting and making bad hospital jokes.

Very soon after, the doctor returned to see how he was doing. Without a doubt, I saw that bright, shiny halo over his head. Here was a man, who by laying-on of hands – and scalpels, sutures, cardiopulmonary bypass machine and anesthesia – was able to perform a miracle. My husband was sitting there with a smile on his face.

As time passed, Stephen recovered, and our family regained its equilibrium. I realized that in the same way that some of us get up and go to the office, deliver mail, plan estates, fill prescriptions, teach high school math or manage capital campaigns, a surgeon performs an average of seven procedures a week, 40 weeks a year. This is what s/he does. That they save and change lives goes with the territory.

I make no claim to walking on water; I will certainly leave that to others. The point about this whole "vision thing" is that, if we are lucky, it is what we follow, what we do. A clear and compelling mission and vision inspire, engage and connect an array of individuals in an endless range of roles and possibilities. It incorporates altruism, self-fulfillment and recognition, with a focus on and benefit to others. It allows us to exercise our own social contract with the world at large.

That is what is important to those individuals who are fortunate enough to choose their life's work. Of course, it's about us, but it is also about others. It's about doing and being something meaningful and different – not better, but different.

It's a difference that makes a difference.

What are the ways in which your own work and that of your organization truly reflects your vision?

SELECTED REFERENCES

American Productivity and Quality Center. 2004. What is Benchmarking?: iSixSigma.

Axelrod, R., and M. D. Cohen. 1999. *Harnessing complexity: Organizational implications of a scientific frontier.* New York: The Free Press.

Bar-Yam, Yaneer. *Concepts in Complex Adaptive Systems.* New England Complex Systems Institute 2007 [cited. Available from http://necsi.edu/guide/concepts/.

Bennis, Warren, and Joan Goldsmith. 2003. *Learning to Lead: A Workbook on Becoming a Leader.* New York: Basic Books.

Bennis, Warren, and Burt Nanus. 1985. *Leaders: The Strategies for Taking Charge.* New York: Harper & Row.

Benton, D. A. 1999. *Secrets of a CEO Coach.* New York: McGraw Hill.

Block, Peter. 1993. *Choosing Service over Self-interest.* San Francisco: Berrett-Koehler.

———. 2003. *The Answer to How is Yes: Acting on What Matters.* San Francisco: Berrett-Koehler.

Bolman, Lee G., and Terrence E. Deal. 1991. *Reframing the Organization.* San Francisco: Jossey-Bass.

Book, Esther Wachs. 2000. *Why the Best Man for the Job is a Woman*. New York: Harper Business.

Bossidy, Larry, and Ram Charan. 2002. *Execution: The Discipline of Getting Thing Done*. New York: Crown Business.

Bridges, William. 1980. *Making Sense of Life's Changes*. Reading, MA: Perseus.

———. 2003. *Managing Transitions: Making the Most of Change*. Reading, MA: Da Capo.

Broom, Michael F., and Donald C. Klein. 1995. *Power: The Infinite Game*. Amherst, MA: HRD Press.

Chase, Richard B., Nicholas J. Aquilano, and F. Robert Jacobs. 2001. *Operations Management for Competitive Advantage*. Boston: McGraw-Hill Irwin.

Cohn, Jeffrey M., Rakesh Khurana, and Laura Reeves. 2005. Growing Talent as if Your Business Depended on It. *Harvard Business Review* (October 2005).

Collins, James C., and Jerry I. Porras. 1994. *Built to Last: Successful Habits of Visionary Companies*. New York: Harper Business.

Cooperrider, David L., and Diana Whitney. 2006. *Appreciative Inquiry: A Positive Revolution in Change*. San Francisco: Barrett-Koehler.

Cowles, Thomas R. 2004. Criteria for Lessons Learned. In *Annual SMMI Technology Conference and User Group*. Denver, CO.

Critchley, Robert K. 2002. *Rewired, Rehired, or Retired? A Global Guide for the Experienced Worker*. San Francisco, CA: Jossey-Bass/Pfeiffer.

Dooley, Kevin. 2002. Organizational complexity. In *International encyclopedia of business and management* London: Thompson Learning.

Drucker, Peter F. 1992. *Managing the Non-Profit Organization*. New York, NY: Harper Collins.

———. 2001. *The Concept of the Corporation*. New Brunswick, NJ: Transaction Publishers.

Eiseley, Loren. 1979. *The Star Thrower*. New York: Harvest Books.

Elsdon, Ron. 2003. *Affiliation in the Workplace*. Westport, CT: Praeger.

Eoyang, Glenda H. 1997. *Coping with Chaos: Seven Simple Tools*. Circle Pines, MN: Lagumo.

———, ed. 2003. *Voices from the Field: An Introduction to Human Systems Dynamics*. Circle Pines, MN: Human Systems Dynamics Institute.

———. 2004. The Practitioner's Landscape. In *E:CO [Online]*.

Eoyang, Glenda H., and A. Weisberg. 1998. *Creative Chaos* [cited. Available from http://www.hsdinstitute.org/e-Clarity/asp_ freeform_0001/user_documents//MMAC.pdf

Esty, Katharine, Richard Griffin, and Marcie Schorr Hirsch. 1995. *Workplace Diversity*. Holbrook, MA: Adams Media.

Feldman, Mark L., and Michael F. Spratt. 1999. *Five Frogs on a Log: A CEO's Field Guide to Accelerating the Transition in Mergers, Acquisitions and Gut Wrenching Change*. New York: Harper Business.

Flach, Frederic. 1988. *Resilience: Discovering a New Strength at Times of Stress*. New York: Fawcett Columbine.

Floyd, Steven W., and Bill Woolridge. 1996. *The Strategic Middle Manager: How to Create and Sustain Competitive Advantage*. San Francisco: Jossey-Bass.

Gell-Mann, Murray. 1994. *The Quark and the Jaguar*. New York: W. H. Freeman and Company.

Gilligan, Carol. 1982. *In a Different Voice*. Cambridge: Harvard University Press.

Gladwell, Malcolm. 2000. *The Tipping Point: How Little Things Can Make a Big Difference*. Boston: Little, Brown and Company.

Gleick, James. 1987. *Chaos: Making a New Science*. New York: Penguin Books.

Goldstein, Jeffrey. 1994. *The Unshackled Organization*. Portland, OR: Productivity Press.

Goleman, Daniel, Richard Boyatzis, and Annue McKee. 2002. *Primal Leadership: Realizing the Power of Emotional Intelligence*. Boston: Harvard Business School Press.

Hart, E. Wayne, and Karen Kirkland. 2001. *Using your Executive Coach*. Greensboro, NC: Center for Creative Leadership.

Harvard Business School Press, ed. 2000. *HBR on Work and Life Balance*. Boston: Harvard Business Review.

Hersey, Paul, Ken Blanchard, and Dewey E. Johnson. 2007. *Management of Organizational Behavior: Leading Human Resources*. New York: Prentice Hall.

Hesselbein, Frances, and Marshall Goldstein. 2006. *The Leader of the Future 2 : Visions, Strategies, and Practices for the New Era Leader to Leader Institute Series*. San Francisco: John Wiley and Sons.

Holladay, Royce. 2004. It's About Voice: Building Productive, Respectful Relationships in the Workplace. In *Human Systems Dynamics Professional Certification Training*. St. Paul, MN.

———. 2005. Simple Rules: Organizational DNA. *OD Practitioner* 37 (4).

Hudson, Frederic M. 1999. *The Handbook of Coaching*. San Francisco: Jossey-Bass.

Jaworski, Joseph. 1998. *Synchronicity: The Inner Path of Leadership*. San Francisco: Berrett-Koehler.

Johnson, Barry. 1996. *Polarity Management: Identifying and Managing Unsolvable Problems*. Amherst, MA: HRD Press.

Kaplan, Robert S., and David P. Norton. 1996. *The Balanced Scorecard: Translating Strategy into Action*. Boston: Harvard Business School Press.

———. 2006. *Alignment: Using the Balanced Scorecard to Create Corporate Synergies* Boston: Harvard Business School Press.

———. 2008. *Execution Premium: Linking Strategy to Operations for Competitive Advantage* Cambridge: Harvard Business School Press.

Katzenbach, Jon R., and Douglas K. Smith. 1993. *The Wisdom of Teams*. New York: Harper Collings Publishers, Inc.

Kaye, Beverly, and Sharon Jordan-Evans. 2003. *Love It Don't Leave It: 26 Ways to Get What You Want at Work*. San Francisco: Berrett-Koehler.

Keary, Deb. 2003. Put Performance Reviews Where They Belong: In Your Routine: Society for Human Resource Management.

Ken Keyes, Jr. 1984. *The Hundredth Monkey*. 2nd ed: Devorss & Co.

Kotter, John P. 1996. *Leading Change*. Boston: Harvard Business School Press.

Ledford, Courtney, Nancy R. Lockwood, Steve Williams, and Nicole Gray. 2008. Leadership Competencies: Society for Human Resource Management.

Lewin, Roger. 1992. *Life at the Edge of Chaos*. New York: Macmillan.

Lombardo, Michael M., and Robert W. Eichenger. 2000. *For Your Improvement*. Minneapolis: Lominger Limited, Inc.

Maxwell, John C. 2006. *The 360 Degree Leader: Developing Your Influence from Anywhere in the Organization*. Nashville, TN: Thomas Nelson.

McNamara, Carter. 2007. Strategic Planning in Non-profit or For-profit Organizations. In *Field Guide to Non-profit Strategic Planning and Facilitation*.

———. 2008. Management Development Planning. In *Field Guide to Non-profit Strategic Planning and Facilitation*.

Mintzberg, Henry, Joseph B. Lampel, James B. Quinn, and Sumantra Ghosal. 2002. *The Strategy Process*. New York: Prentice Hall.

Morgan, Gareth. 1997. *Imaginization. New Mindsets for Seeing, Organizing and Managing*. San Francisco: Barrett-Koehler Publishers, Inc.

National Alliance of Caregiving. 2004 [cited. Available from http://www.familycaregiving101.org/assist/.

National Family Caregivers Association. 2002. *Family Caregiving 101*. National Family Caregivers Association. Kensington, MD.

National Institute for Occupational Health and Safety. *Stress at Work*. Centers for Disease Control and Prevention 2008 [cited. Available from http://www.cdc.gov/niosh/topics/stress/.

Ogilvy, James A. 2002. *Creating Better Futures: Scenario Planning As a Tool for A Better Tomorrow*. London: Oxford University Press.

O'Hara-Devereaux, Mary. 2004. *Navigating the Badlands: Thriving in the Decade of Radical Transformation*. San Francisco: Jossey-Bass.

Olson, Edwin E., and Glenda H. Eoyang. 2001. *Facilitating Organizational Change: Lessons from Complexity Science*. San Francisco: Jossey-Bass/Pfeiffer.

O'Neill, Mary Beth. 2000. *Executive Coaching with Heart and Backbone*. San Francisco: Jossey-Bass.

Osborne, David, and Ted Garbler. 1993. *Reinventing Government. How the Entrepreneurial Spirit is Transforming the Public Sector*. Reading, MA: Addison-Wesley.

Patton, Michael Q. 1997. *Utilization-Focused Evaluation*. Thousand Oaks, CA: Sage.

Porter, Michael E. 1985. *Competitive Advantage: Creating and Sustaining Superior Performance.* New York: The Free Press.

———. 1996. What is Strategy? *Harvard Business Review* (October 1996).

Quinn, Robert E. Moments of Greatness: Entering the Fundamental State of Leadership. *Harvard Business Review* (July - August 2005).

Rogers, Everett M. 1983. *Diffusion of Innovations.* New York: The Free Press.

Schmitt, Bernd. 2003. *Customer Experience Management: A Revolutionary Approach to Connecting with Your Customers.* New York: Wiley.

Senge, Peter, C. Otto Scharmer, Joseph Jaworski, and Betty Sue Flowers. 2004. *Presence: An Exploration of Profound Change in People, Organizations and Society.* New York: Doubleday.

Senge, Peter M., Bryan Smith, Nina Kruschwitz, Joe Laur, and Sara Schley. *The Necessary Revolution: How Individuals and Organizations are Working Together to Create a Sustainable World.* Doubleday Currency 2008 [cited. Available from http://www.petzinger.com/alive.shtml.

Sessa, Valerie I., and Jodi J. Taylor. 2000. *Executive Selection: Strategies for Success.* San Francisco: Jossey-Bass and Center for Creative Leadership.

Sibley, David, and Julia Yoshida. 2002. Spotting Patterns on the Fly. *Harvard Business Review.*

Smith, Elizabeth A. 1995. *Creating Productive Organizations: Developing Your Work Force.* Delray Beach, FL: St. Lucie Press.

Stacey, Ralph D. 1992. *Managing the Unknowable.* San Francisco, CA: Jossey Bass.

———. 1996. *Complexity and Creativity in Organizations.* San Francisco: Berrett-Koehler.

Stack, Linda. 2004. Learn How to Recognize and Combat Desk Rage: Society for Human Resource Management.

Stern, Joel M., and John S. Shiely. 2001. *The EVA Challenge.* New York: John Wiley & Sons.

Sweeney, Linda Booth. 2001. *When a Butterfly Sneezes.* Waltham, MA: Pegasus Communications.

Treacy, Michael, and Fred Wiersema. 1997. *The Discipline of Market Leaders.* Reading, MA: Perseus

U.S. Small Business Administration. *Small Business Planner* 2008 [cited. Available from http://www.sba.gov/smallbusinessplanner/index.html.

Wexler, Phillip S., W. A. Adams, and Emil Bohn. 1993. *The Quest for Quality: Prescriptions for Achieving Service Quality.* New York: St. Martin's Griffin.

Whitney, Diana, David Cooperrider, Amanda Trosten-Bloom, and Brian S. Kaplan. 2002. *Encyclopedia of Positive Questions.* Euclid, OH: Lakeshore Communications.

Wiersema, Fred. 1996. *Customer Intimacy.* Santa Monica, CA: Knowledge Exchange.

Woodward, Nancy Hatch. 2006. Making the Most of Team Building: Society for Human Resource Management.

Zimmerman, Brenda, Curt Lindberg, and Paul Plsek. 1998. *Edgeware: Insights from Complexity Science for Health Care Leaders*. Irving, TX: VHA, Inc.

ABOUT THE AUTHOR

Mallary Tytel is president and founder of Healthy Workplaces, a national consulting firm that focuses on best practices in leadership development, coaching, organizational culture and strategic thinking for individuals and organizations.

She is the former CEO of an international nonprofit behavioral health, human resource development and training corporation; has served as a key advisor to senior-level civilian and military personnel within the U.S. Department of Defense; has provided oversight and coordination for three Congressionally-mandated pilot programs in 16 communities across the country; and created and delivered an innovative training program to over 40 military communities worldwide. An expert source, Mallary is often quoted in the media, including the New York Times, Entrepreneur Magazine and the Chronicle of Philanthropy and has appeared on CNBC and ABC World News This Morning. She is also a regular contributor to BusinessWeek.com.

Mallary has a Ph.D. in Public Health Promotion and Organizational Systems from the Union Institute and University and an M.B.A. from the University of Connecticut. She is a Certified Executive Coach, Registered Corporate Coach and Mediator, as well as an Adjunct faculty member and executive coach for the Center for Creative Leadership. In her spare time she is chairman of the board of the Prevention Think Tank™, which she co-founded, writes and mentors budding women entrepreneurs.

You may contact Mallary at mtytel@healthyworkplaces.com or www.healthyworkplaces.com.

Printed in the United States
138253LV00002B/7/P